ons, we have organized the Parkw
th to north) order by milepost:

Kaintuck Boatmen and the Postal Road

Archeology and Native Americans

Prehistoric Sites

The Choctaw

The Chickasaw

Guide to the
NATCHEZ TRACE PARKWAY

F. Lynne Bachleda

Dedicated to

Geneva Sue DeButy Smith

Guide to the
NATCHEZ TRACE PARKWAY

F. Lynne Bachleda

MENASHA RIDGE PRESS
BIRMINGHAM, ALABAMA

Copyright © 2005 F. Lynne Bachleda
All rights reserved
Printed in China
Published by Menasha Ridge Press
Distributed by Publishers Group West
First edition, second printing 2007

Library of Congress Cataloging-in-Publication Data
Bachleda, F. Lynne
  Guide to the Natchez Trace Parkway / F. Lynne Bachleda
     p. cm.
  Includes bibliographical references (p. 136).
ISBN 10: 0-89732-595-8
ISBN 13: 978-0-89732-595-0

  1. Natchez Trace Parkway—Guidebooks. 2. Natchez
Trace—Guidebooks. 3. Automobile travel—Natchez
Trace Parkway—Guidebooks. I. Title.

F217.N37B33 2005
971.62—dc22   2004060987

Cover and interior design by Grant Tatum
Cover photo © Alex Demyan
All interior photographs © F. Lynne Bachleda
Cartography by Steve Jones

Menasha Ridge Press
P.O. Box 43673
Birmingham, AL 35243
www.menasharidge.com

Table of Contents

Table of Contents

Natchez Trace Parkway Map Legend

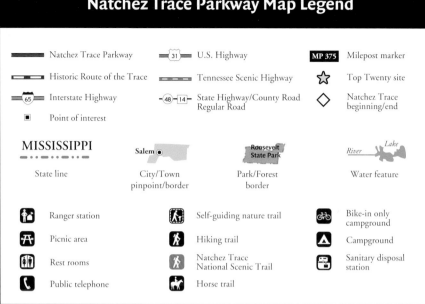

Natchez Trace Parkway		U.S. Highway		MP 375	Milepost marker
Historic Route of the Trace		Tennessee Scenic Highway		☆	Top Twenty site
Interstate Highway		State Highway/County Road Regular Road		◇	Natchez Trace beginning/end
Point of interest					

MISSISSIPPI	Salem ●	Roosevelt State Park	River / Lake
State line	City/Town pinpoint/border	Park/Forest border	Water feature

Ranger station	Self-guiding nature trail	Bike-in only campground
Picnic area	Hiking trail	Campground
Rest rooms	Natchez Trace National Scenic Trail	Sanitary disposal station
Public telephone	Horse trail	

Key to Icons in Text

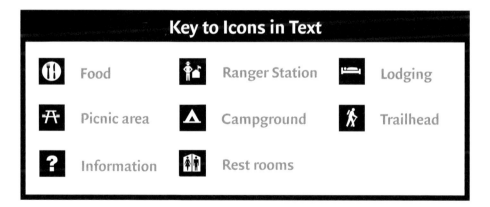

Food		Ranger Station		Lodging
Picnic area		Campground		Trailhead
Information		Rest rooms		

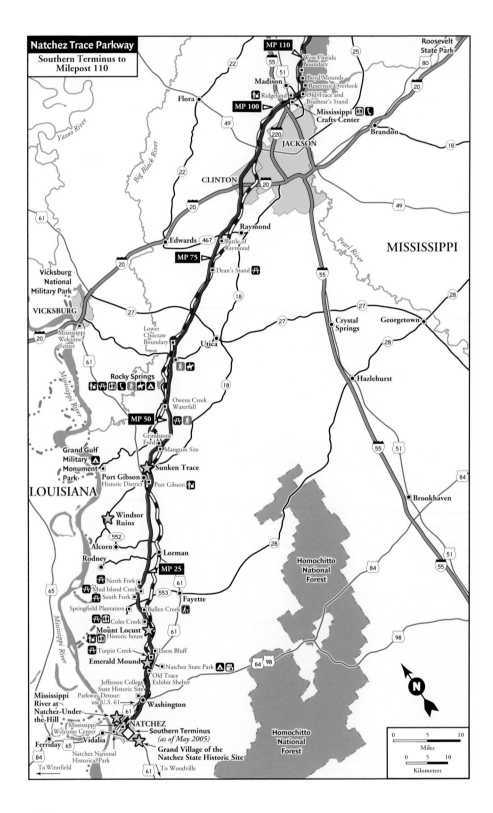

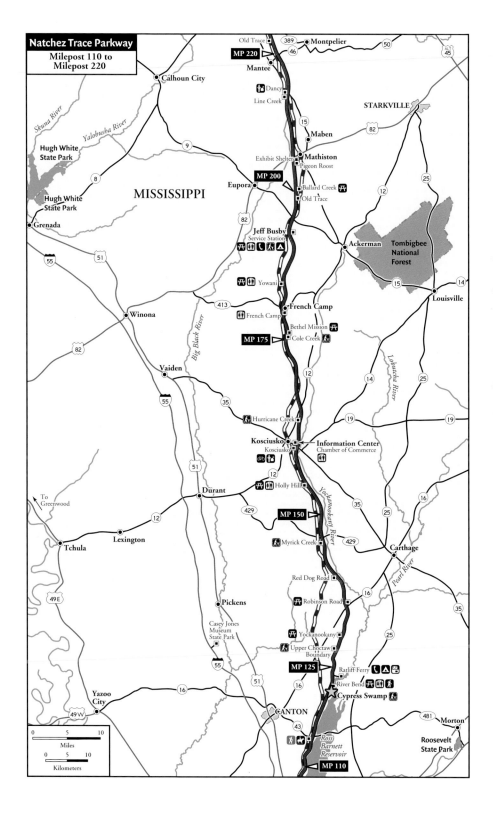

Natchez Trace Parkway

Milepost 110 to
Milepost 220

MISSISSIPPI

Hugh White State Park

Hugh White State Park

Tombigbee National Forest

Roosevelt State Park

Ross Barnett Reservoir

Casey Jones Museum State Park

Skuna River
Yalobusha River
Big Black River
Yockanookany River
Lobutcha River
Pearl River

Montpelier
MP 220
Mantee
Calhoun City
STARKVILLE
Dancy
Line Creek
Maben
Mathiston
Exhibit Shelter
Pigeon Roost
MP 200
Eupora
Ballard Creek
Old Trace
Ackerman
Grenada
Jeff Busby
Service Station
Yowani
Louisville
French Camp
French Camp
Winona
Bethel Mission
MP 175
Cole Creek
Vaiden
Hurricane Creek
Kosciusko
Information Center
Chamber of Commerce
Kosciusko
Durant
Holly Hill
To Greenwood
MP 150
Myrick Creek
Lexington
Tchula
Carthage
Red Dog Road
Pickens
Robinson Road
Yockanookany
Upper Choctaw Boundary
MP 125
Yazoo City
Ratliff Ferry
River Bend
Cypress Swamp
CANTON
MP 110
Morton

Old Trace

To Greenwood

0   5   10
Miles

0   5   10
Kilometers

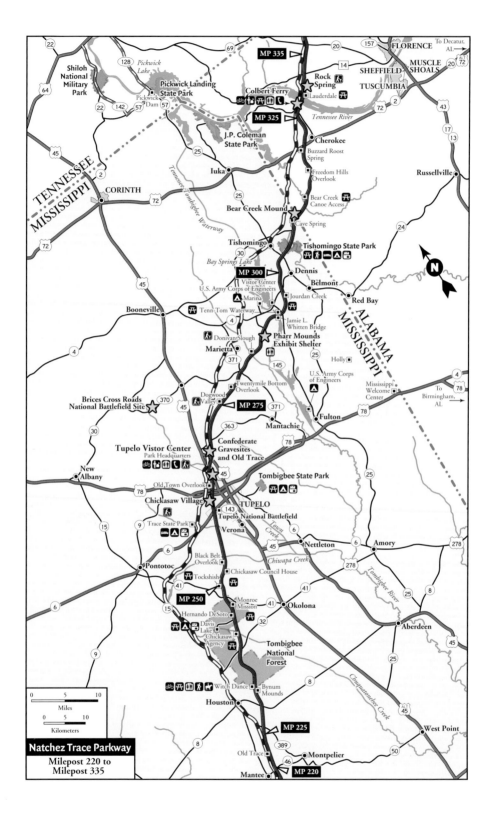

Natchez Trace Parkway
Milepost 220 to
Milepost 335

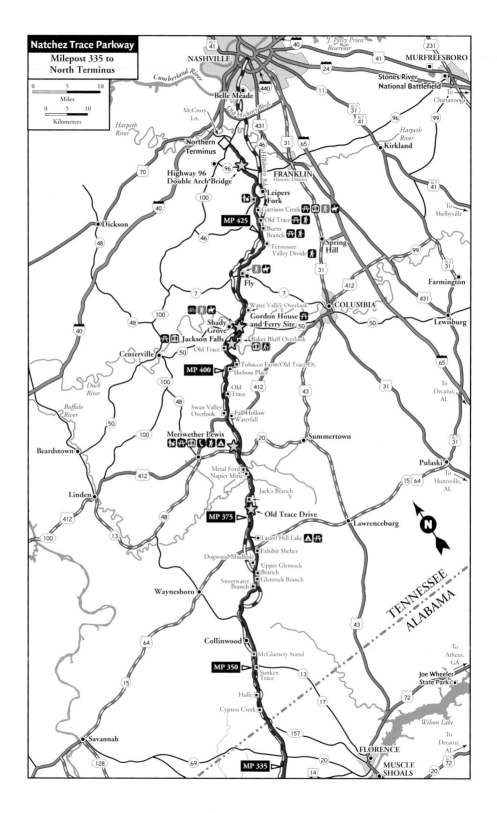

(*On page xiv*) **Cypress Creek, near the Tennessee and Alabama state lines, is one of the Parkway's many** relaxing opportunities to enjoy the outdoors

Acknowledgments

The support of the National Park Service (NPS) staff at the Tupelo headquarters has been invaluable to this project. Kathy Brock, now at Harpers Ferry Center, welcomed the project from the beginning, as did Donna Gregory, who also loaned me reference materials. In particular, Visitor Center Supervisor Ernie Price has been a substantial help in thinking through this book, as well as helping me keep my facts straight. The NPS Teacher's Information Packet was a great source to which I turned with frequency and, often, relief. My gratitude goes also to LaDonna Brown, Brian Gills, and Lynda Tinsley. The entire staff shares an uncommon passion and dedication, and they are an inspiration and a tribute to the life of the Trace.

My thanks also go to those who have previously written about the Trace and the Natchez Trace Parkway. Please seek out their fine works in "Resources" (p. 135) at the end of this book. In particular, Ilene Cornwell, committed writer and historian, first drew my attention to the Trace in the early 1980s. Her pioneering work and her pure love of the Trace and its stories were guiding lights.

It is my pleasure to acknowledge the aid of Ellen Morefield, who drove the Parkway in northern Mississippi, Alabama, and Tennessee so I could observe, think, and write. Your companionship and support continue to lighten my load and brighten my path in so many ways. Thank you for your love, sustenance, and patience.

My thanks also go to Christina Crowe, a highly skilled editor, for her perseverance and improvements made to the text.

Finally, I gladly acknowledge my gratitude to Geneva Smith. Neevie, honey, it was you who led me to glimpse the native spirit and the pioneer heart. These gifts helped me greatly to fall in love with the Trace. Blessings, forever.

Introduction

• •

OVERVIEW

*In 1962, when Dr. Dawson Phelps presented himself at
the Great Smokies information desk, to the inquiry
"Where are you from?" he confessed with some pride to
being a Park Service man stationed at the Natchez Trace.
To his astonishment the ranger replied, "I certainly feel
sorry for you!" To Dr. Phelps's "Why?" the ranger replied,
"Because you have nothing for visitors to see."*

—Dr. John Mohlhenrich's rewrite
of Dr. Dawson Phelps's 1965
Administrative History of the Natchez Trace

That Smoky Mountain ranger could not have been more
wrong. Most federal parks or landmarks are devoted to a
limited number of themes. The graceful Natchez Trace
Parkway "ribbon of time," however, has many threads. It
can transport you back 9,000 years to the time of Paleo
indian hunters; drop you into a Civil War battle; urge
you to contemplate "the Nile of the Western hemisphere;" encourage you to empathize with foot-weary

nineteenth-century travelers yearning for home; and teach you about contemporary conservation farming practices. The historical riches, cultural avenues, and exploratory possibilities of the Natchez Trace Parkway are numerous.

This park's natural beauty doesn't come from dramatic mountainous overlooks. Instead, you will find mostly flat terrain rendered in a balanced, subtle palette. In the spring, roadside stretches of clover, wildflowers, grassy fields, and dogwood blossoms wave. Summer is often crowned with pure blue skies and a healthy green, divided only by the yellow-striped roadway. In the fall, the soft, gray Spanish moss gives way to the russet of maples and oaks. In winter the sturdy dark green of mature cedars takes on promising significance. The road alternately holds you in the close embrace of its shady refuge or shoots you into the light-filled pastures and croplands. This is a hypnotic environment, a soothing melody of forest and field.

The most famous period for this path was from around 1790 to 1820, when it served as one of the primary passageways through the southwest territory of what was then a relatively new country. Farmers, boatmen, diplomats, ladies, preachers, bandits, soldiers, murderers, and slaves tramped it to travel between Nashville, Tennessee and Natchez, Mississippi. By 1800

National Park Service sign toward the northern end of the Natchez Trace Parkway

it was also a United States postal route ridden on horse-back by courageous men who risked their lives at break-neck speeds. But the Trace has been around for much, much longer than a mere two centuries.

This long, narrow federal preserve can be both uncomplicated and complex. The well-maintained road is relatively straight for most of its 444 miles. The twists and turns do not arise so much from the pavement as from the overlay of the lives of those to whom the Trace has meant so many different things.

The Natchez Trace Parkway asks you to slow down. Driving at 50 miles per hour is a legal requirement on most stretches. It will also help you relax and notice the Parkway's many sights. Using your imagination, you can replicate some of the same experiences that others before you have had here for millennia. After all, many of the vistas have not changed substantially. Ultimately, this is the affirming power of the Trace: along this distance, powerfully strong human and natural links still exist across time.

"

*the Natchez Trace Parkway
asks you to slow down*

"

WHAT AND WHERE IS THE NATCHEZ TRACE?

The Natchez Trace Parkway is not laid precisely over what the interpretive signs refer to as "the Old Trace." In fact, there is no single course that was "the Old Trace."

In *The Natchez Trace: Indian Trail to Parkway,* author Dawson Phelps explains:

> Historically, there were two, possibly three, Natchez Traces, each having a different origin and purpose. The first was the Indian trail. The second, the "Boatman's Trail," was beaten out by men from the Ohio Valley returning to their homes from trading expeditions to Spanish Louisiana. The third was a road which was opened up by the United States Government to facilitate overland travel between Natchez and Nashville. . . .

The modern concept that a road follows a fixed route does not apply to the Natchez Trace. During the short time that the road was a major line of communication, its location shifted to meet the rapidly changing needs of the southwestern frontier. Only rarely do all of the vari-ous locations coincide, making it possible to say, "This is the Natchez Trace."

Congress authorized a survey of the old Natchez Trace for possible construction of a Natchez Trace Park-way on May 21, 1936. Seventy-one years later—as of

May 18, 2005—the last section around Jackson, Mississippi was scheduled for completion, making the Parkway one seamless ride from Natchez, Mississippi to Pasquo, Tennessee, about 15 miles southwest of downtown Nashville. The federal lands that border the Parkway average about 412.5 feet on each side of the Parkway for a total of about 52,000 acres.

THE VISITOR CENTER

There is only one visitor center, in Tupelo, Mississippi, slightly north of the Parkway's midpoint.

Natchez Trace Parkway Visitor Center
2680 Natchez Trace Parkway
Tupelo, MS 38804-9718

Open year-round except for Christmas Day, 8 a.m.–5 p.m.
(800) 305-7417 or (662)680-4027
www.nps.gov/natr

TOUGH OLD TRACES

This early interstate road-building venture—snake-infested, mosquito beset, robber-haunted, Indian-traveled forest path—was lamented by the pious, cursed by the impious, and tried everyone's strength and patience.

—National Park Service sign at
Sunken Trace at milepost 350.5

Until the 1830s, when the reliability of steamboat travel north on the Mississippi River made it somewhat obsolete, the Natchez Trace was a well-traveled road. This was especially true from about 1790 to 1810.

As you cruise smoothly along the Parkway, imagine setting out to walk north from Natchez, nearly 500 miles over twisting, brambly, muddy trails that sometimes disappeared into thick woods or were blocked by large, storm-fallen trees. Having traversed swamps, creeks, and bayous, you still faced the challenge of crossing the Tennessee River and climbing the route's largest ridges. There were critters aplenty, and although danger from the attack of wild animals presented more of a mental hazard than an actual one, 1797 Trace traveler Francis Bailey wrote that he saw enough wolves, bear, and deer to keep night fires going.

Probably the greatest danger of travel through the wilderness was the possibility of becoming sick or having an injury too severe to reach medical attention on time, if at all. The aggravations didn't have to be life threatening to make life miserable. Bailey, and no doubt numerous others, suffered from a severe allergy to poison ivy, a plant still abundant today on the Old Trace. His legs were so swollen he had to make moccasins to replace his snug boots before he could continue his journey. Insects, especially during periods of wet weather, presented another constant discomfort to the travelers.

Petty larceny and horse theft were common occurrences in the Indian country. According to the National Park Service (NPS), horse stealing was the most prevalent form of robbery among the natives. The wise traveler anticipating a trip through the wilderness packed iron hobbles to fasten together the legs of his horse so it could neither stray nor be stolen. Often horses were stolen only to be returned by the thieves a short time later in order to claim a reward.

As if all these challenges were not enough, in the early years of the nineteenth century the Trace came to be infested by a daring band of outlaws. Generally very cruel, these mostly white and some native bandits and murderers were a specter of terror for all those traveling through the wilderness. Merchants and traders returning from the Natchez country laden with the profits of their sales made especially easy prey.

The people who survived the walk home proved themselves to be lucky and hardy, to say the least.

> " bandits and murderers were a specter of terror for all those traveling through the wilderness "

THE BIRTH AND DEATH OF THE NATCHEZ TRACE AS A ROAD

> *This old road, with its distinctive landmarks, forests, cane-brakes, ridges, and swamps recalls an early and heroic chapter in our national epic.*
>
> —Dawson Phelps, in
> *An Administrative History of the Natchez Trace Parkway*

The Natchez Trace began as ancient animal trails worn by creatures heading toward the salt springs in what is now Nashville. The passage and its parts were variously called the "Chickasaw Trail," "Path to the Choctaw Nation," "Boatman's Trail," "Natchez Road," "Nashville Road, " "Mail Road," and even "Cumberland Road." It acquired the name "Natchez Trace" sometime after its heavy use dwindled in the 1820s.

The Trace passes through lands that the Natchez, Choctaw, and Chickasaw nations used primarily for dwelling, farming, and hunting. Hernando de Soto claimed this territory for Spain in 1540–1541. By 1798 the Spanish relinquished their claims north of the 31st parallel that cuts across the Deep South in southern Mississippi. This freed the port of Natchez to open more widely to Mississippi River trade. The influx of boatmen who needed a way home did much to publicize the route.

As commerce and land attracted more settlers, the U.S. Government needed a quicker way to communicate with the Mississippi Territory. So in 1800, it established the postal route between Nashville and Natchez. Indian treaties permitted the establishment of a road, and in 1801 the project began under the command of notorious General James Wilkinson.

In 1806 Congress appropriated $6,000 to improve the road, probably to mollify the complaints of the postal riders. No maintenance money, however, was provided, and, to the dismay of its many travelers, the road soon returned to its rugged form. Military use of the route peaked during the war years of 1812–1815, when Andrew Jackson traveled the Trace with his men. After his victory at the Battle of New Orleans, the military needs for the road ceased and so did much congressional interest in it.

Still, the postal riders continued their brave journeys along the old road, and by 1816 there were three mail deliveries a week. The government began to rely more on the steamboat to carry the mail in the 1820s.

THE RESURRECTION OF THE NATCHEZ TRACE AS A PARKWAY

It requires no stretch of the imagination to look back upon a time when the Natchez Trace was practically unknown to the people of Mississippi . . . But with pardonable pride, we claim for the Mississippi Society of the Daughters of the American Revolution the credit for awakening general public interest.

—Mrs. A. F. Fox of West Point, Mississippi, 1910

After about 85 years of disuse, the rebirth of the Trace likely started with a 1905 article by John Swain entitled "The Natchez Trace" that appeared in *Everybody's Magazine.* That same year, a member of the Mississippi chapter of the Daughters of the American Revolution (DAR), Mrs. Egbert Jones of Holly Springs, Mississippi, proposed that the DAR commemorate the Trace by placing an interpretive marker in every county through which the Trace ran. They enlisted their sister organizations in Tennessee and Alabama to complement their efforts. The LaSalle chapter placed a monument in Tishomingo in 1908, and the Mississippi chapter placed one overlooking the Mississippi River at Natchez in 1909.

When the lure of history failed to ignite more public interest in the Trace's preservation, the DAR changed tactics toward the public's desire for good roads. The "Pave the Trace" campaign, formally inaugurated in 1916 by the Natchez Chamber of Commerce, was short lived, but it was a start. For decades the Mississippi DAR continued their efforts to have the Trace recognized. Marker dedications were occasions for speeches, which tended to draw reporters and politicians. Interest

A smooth, serene stretch of road along the Natchez Trace Parkway

in the Trace began to grow in serious historical journals and in newspaper articles.

A January, 1932 address at one of the dedications by Thomas A. Bailey, who went on to become governor of Mississippi, was another turning point for the Trace. As a result, Ned Lee, editor of the *Webster Progress* newspaper, became interested and assigned columnist Jim Walton to research and write about the Trace in his "Nits and Tidbits" column. In August 1933 Walton suggested to Mississippi Congressman Jeff Busby that he introduce a bill in Congress to survey the Old Trace.

The timing was right as the country was looking for New Deal Public Works Administration projects that would benefit the public, stimulate economically depressed areas, and provide work for people in desperate need of a job. Also, the National Recovery Act of 1933 called for a comprehensive system of public works that included highways and parkways. Backed by much local support, Busby introduced two bills in the U.S. House of Representatives. The first would authorize $50,000 to survey the Old Trace, and the second asked for $25 million to construct the Natchez Trace Parkway. Only the survey money was approved at that time, but on June 30, 1937 construction finally began when three grading permits were issued in Mississippi. On May 18, 1938 the Natchez Trace Parkway, which still had miles and miles to go, was created as a unit of the National Park Service. Federal funding came in fits and starts over the next 60-plus years. May 18, 2005 marks the scheduled conclusion of piecemeal road construction. The Natchez Trace Parkway's legacy continues, however, with the acquisition of new interpretive sites and plans for additional visitor centers.

You can still see DAR markers along the Parkway. Some are so weathered they are hard to read, but they serve as reminders of the good that committed volunteers, along with the help of a few writers, some bureaucrats, and even a politician or two, can achieve.

HOW TO USE THIS GUIDE
The core of this book is Chapter Five, "Sight-seeing by Milepost" (p. 67). It is organized to correspond to the National Park Service's Natchez Trace Parkway map/brochure that is widely available along the Parkway and can be obtained in advance by contacting the visitor center (see information on p. 4). That map has been

"
on May 18, 1938 the Natchez Trace Parkway was created as a unit of the National Park Service
"

replicated in this book on pages viii–xi. The milepost marker system, explained in Chapter Two, "The Nuts and Bolts of Traveling the Trace" (p. 29), correlates the various sights with the Parkway's roadside markers running numerically from south to north. This is the direction the Trace was most often traveled during its busiest years.

"Sight-seeing by Milepost" is also broken down by cities and states, the geographical touchstones with which people are most familiar. With few exceptions, all of the stops in this book are on the map. You are invited to enjoy places that pertain to the Trace story, so we encourage you, for example, to visit downtown Nashville's Tennessee Bicentennial Capitol Mall where ancient animals, who originally trod the Trace's paths, gathered at the sulfur salt spring. Web sites in the "Resources" section of the book (p. 135) can help you find what you want to see in the cities along the Trace.

Every effort has been made to provide you with as much information as possible to help you with your trip, including information on state and federal campgrounds along the way. In lieu of specific hotel, motel, and restaurant listings, you will find a contact list in the "Appendixes" section (p. 141) that can connect you with the most recent information for a given locale.

Most importantly, enjoy your travels on the Trace. It is a truly special place that willingly reveals itself to you if you meet it with an expansive imagination and the gift of your time.

"

most importantly, enjoy your travels on the Trace

"

(On following page)
Trees that have stood watch over the Trace for years still shade the historic roadway

Chapter One

Traveling Your Own Trace

. . . .

"SHOULD WE STOP HERE?"

This is probably the most commonly asked question on the Natchez Trace Parkway. There are about 100 possible milepost stops, so you have a lot of options. Exploring a 200-year-old log cabin; studying a swamp; climbing a prehistoric people's ceremonial mound; honoring fallen soldiers at a Civil War cemetery; hiking an ancient animal path; and visiting the place where Elvis was born are each possibilities in a single day of travel along the Parkway.

In an attempt to sort out the options, we've created some categories to help you key in to the stops that might interest you the most along the way.

PARKWAY CATEGORIES

The most important category is the "Trace Top Twenty." These are the sights, selected in consultation with the National Park Service (NPS), that we don't want you to miss. They represent the best of what the Parkway has to offer. Each is marked on the maps with a star (✪).

The other categories are:

- ▧ **The Old Trace**
- ▧ **Kaintuck Boatmen and the Postal Road**
- ▧ **Archeology and Native Americans**
- ▧ **Natural Wonders**
- ▧ **Civil War and Other Military History**
- ▧ **The Living Trace**
- ▧ **National Park Service (NPS) Information**

The following descriptions will give you a context and understanding for each category.

The Trace Top Twenty

This category naturally has a bit of everything in it, a testament to the Parkway's variety. After indicating the sites in Natchez, we've listed them in ascending (south to north) milepost order for easy reference. Each is marked on the maps with a star (✪). Within Chapter Five, "Sight-seeing by Milepost", (p. 67) you can find more information on each of these highly recommended stops.

1. **The Mississippi River at Natchez-Under-the Hill** (in Natchez) The river is the real genesis of the Trace story, and at this point along its banks you can stand where thousands of "Kaintuck" boatmen unloaded and sold their goods, partied, and began to think about the long walk home along the Natchez Trace. (p. 69)

2. **Grand Village of the Natchez Indians** (in Natchez) This ceremonial site was a political and religious home to the Natchez tribe, a group of people historically linked to the mound builders. Here among the mounds you can contemplate the Natchez's burial rituals, as well as the choice they made that triggered their decimation. (p. 71)

3. **Emerald Mound** (milepost 10.3) Staggering in its size and lingering power, this second-largest Mississippian mound in the United States covers eight acres. Only Cahokia in Ohio is larger. (p. 75)

4. **Mount Locust** (milepost 15.5) The only remaining stand (inn) from the Trace's heyday of heavy traffic at the beginning of the nineteenth century, this restored cabin is one of the oldest buildings in Mississippi. It provides a good look at one of the austere-at-best realities of Trace travel. (p. 77)

5. **Windsor Ruins** (exit at milepost 30.0 or 41.0) For

those who love romantic antebellum architecture, these ghostly, dramatic columns tell a tale of long-gone grandeur, early death, and fiery tragedy for one wealthy Southern family. (pp.79, 81)

6. **Sunken Trace** (milepost 41.5) This is a short section of the Trace, the one pictured on the NPS map cover. Here you get a real sense of the original Trace's eroded, timeworn quality and a hint of how land pirates could have easily ambushed the unsuspecting. (p. 81)

7. **Cypress Swamp** (milepost 122) If your idea of the Deep South is Spanish moss swaying in a slight breeze over swampy marshes where alligators glide, this is where your dreams meet reality. (p. 90)

8. **Chickasaw Village Site** (milepost 261.8) Here your imagination is your key to seeing how native peoples once lived as you tour the outlines of a once-thriving Native American community. (p. 106)

9. **Tupelo Visitor Center and Parkway Headquarters** (milepost 266.0) At the only in-depth information station on the Parkway, you'll find interpretive exhibits, a video presentation, a bookstore and gift shop, and the wonderful NPS staff to help you make the most out of your Natchez Trace trip. (p.106)

10. **Brices Cross Roads National Battlefield** (exit at milepost 266.0) Take this side trip off the Parkway to visit the site where Confederate States of America General Nathan Bedford Forrest waged a battle that is still studied in military schools worldwide. Learn from the past how you can be greatly out-manned, but still out-wit your enemy. (p. 107)

11. **Confederate Graves on the Old Trace** (milepost 269.4) On an easy walk, this serene and poignant line of unknown soldiers' memorials is also a gentle reminder of the many, from all walks of life, who died along the Trace. (p. 109)

12. **Pharr Mounds** (milepost 286.7) This 90-acre panorama has eight ancient mounds. It is one of the largest and most important archeological sites in the mid-South. (p. 110)

13. **Bear Creek Mound** (milepost 308.8) Bear Creek Mound is among the oldest mounds on the Parkway. When you stand here you're amidst the traces of people who used the adjacent village site 9,000 years ago. (p. 112)

"

visit the site where Confederate States of America General Nathan Bedford Forrest waged a battle that is still studied in military schools worldwide

"

14. **Colbert Ferry** (milepost 327.3) The ferry itself is long gone, but you can contemplate the massive strength of the now-dammed Tennessee River and learn what it was like to try to ford it on foot or horseback 200 years ago. (p. 116)

15. **Rock Spring** (milepost 330.2) A jewel of a nature retreat that follows a crystal-clear spring back to its source. (p. 118)

16. **Old Trace Drive** (milepost 375.8) The easiest way to enjoy and appreciate 2.5 miles of the original roadway from the comfort of your car. This one, however, is not for travel trailers or RVs. (p. 120)

17. **Meriwether Lewis** (milepost 385.9) Visit the gravesite of one of America's most promising young heroes, he of Lewis and Clark fame. No one knows if he was murdered or committed suicide here on the Trace. (p. 121)

18. **Jackson Falls** (milepost 404.7) A mildly challenging, short hike here will reward you with the sight of refreshing falls rippling down a high limestone bank. (p. 125)

19. **Gordon House and Ferry Site** (milepost 407.7) One of only two active Trace-era structures still standing, this is the nearly 200-year-old home of John Gordon and Dolly Cross Gordon. Dolly managed a 1,500-acre plantation, raised ten children, and lived here for 40 years after John died. She passed away in 1859, but you can still sense her vigorous legacy here. (p. 127)

20. **Highway 96 Double Arch Bridge** (milepost est. 438.0) Soaring arches span a quiet valley in this breakthrough feat of engineering that has won 13 design awards. (p. 130)

The Old Trace

these natural trails attracted centuries of Native Americans in search of game

. . . we got safe across [the Duck River]. On the opposite shore we found it difficult to rejoin the path which led to our destined port, as there were so many paths crossing and recrossing each other.

—Francis Bailey, Trace traveler in 1797, who wrote *Early Travels in the Tennessee Country*

The historic route of the Old Trace, which only sometimes runs concurrently with the modern Parkway, was never a single path running from Natchez to Nashville.

These natural trails attracted centuries of Native Americans in search of game. In time, the Trace became a meandering mish-mash that was often obscured by weather's effects.

More than 120 years passed between the heyday of the Trace as a foot-and-bridle path, around 1810, and the Congressionally authorized survey to reclaim it. When you take note of what is marked on the map of the Natchez Trace Parkway as the "historic route of the Trace," understand that in many cases you are looking at an approximation.

There are several opportunities to walk or drive parts of the Old Trace. Most sections are short and take only five to ten minutes to explore. The most visually romantic section is probably "Sunken Trace" at milepost 41.5. At mileposts 198.6 and 221.4 the Old Trace crosses the Parkway, so you get a first-hand look at the meandering quality of the original route. At milepost 350.5 you can discern where the road was rerouted to avoid mud holes. Drivers (except those pulling trailers) can enjoy a 2.5-mile driving section starting at milepost 375.8. The Old Trace stop at milepost 397.4 permits you to walk 2 miles to the Garrison Creek pull-off. One of the longer sections is at milepost 403.7, where the path is about 0.6 miles out-and-back.

There is no substitute for examining all the sections of the Old Trace that you can.

Kaintuck Boatmen and the Postal Road

*Bands of travelers moved closer together, with intenser [sic]
caution, through the glassy tunnels of the Trace, for all the
proportion went away, and they followed one another like
insects going at dawn through the heavy grass . . .*

—Eudora Welty, *First Love*

Traffic on the Mississippi River transformed the Natchez
Trace into one of America's most important historic
roads. As increasing numbers of settlers pushed into the
Ohio River Valley in the late 1700s, they began to look
to the Mississippi and Ohio rivers to get their goods to
market. Using flatboats and sometimes keel boats, these
farmers became part-time boatmen.

Floating downstream was precarious, but pulling or
rowing a boat upstream even more difficult and dangerous. Eventually, boatmen who stopped at Natchez
learned of an overland route through Indian territory
back to Nashville where they could head home by a less
arduous and risky path. Kentuckians were particularly
prominent among the men who floated downstream on
the Cumberland, Tennessee, Ohio, and Mississippi
Rivers, sold their goods—including the boats for lum-
ber—at Natchez, and then began to walk home. Thus,
the whole group became known as "Kaintucks," regard-
less of their state affiliations.

The approximate distance between Natchez and
Nashville was considered to be more than 500 miles, and
the time required to travel the distance varied consider-
ably. In rare instances, travel on horseback between
Natchez and Nashville could be accomplished in 10 to
12 days, although under normal circumstances approximately 20 days were required. For those traveling on
foot, an average of 25 miles per day was feasible, and the
trip might thus take anywhere from 20 to 30 days. Now
you can travel between Natchez and Nashville in one day.

As the southwestern frontier territory became more
populated, Washington, D.C. bureaucrats developed a
need to communicate with the people living there. So as
boatmen were tramping home, mail began moving along
the Trace. With all this traffic rose the need for lodging
along the Trace. In 1801 the Choctaws and the Chickasaws agreed to permit inns on their lands. Typically these

"stands" had some connection to the Indian tribes if they were on Indian land. Sheboss Place, for example, in Chickasaw country was owned by a native man and his white wife.

In more cases than not, the meals offered at stands consisted of only a mess of mush and milk, some fried bacon, and possibly some fresh meat. Sleeping arrangements generally consisted of the hard floor of the one-room structure, although the traveler always had the option of sleeping outside. Charges for these services varied from 10 cents to 25 cents per person.

These stands, which at one time numbered more than 50, were mostly crude, one-room shelters, but were a welcome site to Trace-weary travelers. Most of the primitive, often hastily built structures are long gone, but the NPS has protected many of the sites where they were located. At Mount Locust, you can tour the lone surviving cabin.

Post riders had to endure all the difficulties of the Trace under the added duress of a tight schedule, which sometimes required that they even ride at night with little regard for personal safety. Groups of travelers tried to band together, keeping to the "safety in numbers" adage. Moving in a group could be extraordinarily slow, however, so a few struck out on their own, praying that nothing deadly would befall them. Oftentimes they were wrong.

Until about 1803, when the federal government cracked down on their activities, bandits were a real problem on the Trace. Solo travelers who were known to be carrying profits from sales in Natchez and New Orleans went alone into the wild territory of the Trace and often met with mayhem.

During the 40 years between 1790 and 1830, the Natchez Trace carried many thousands of homeward-bound boatmen, as well as an assortment of other travelers. With the appearance of steamboats during the mid 1810s, which provided a much easier and safer method of returning home, foot travel over the Trace began to slowly decline. New federal roads, such as the Jackson Military Road that shaved 200 miles off the distance between Nashville and New Orleans, also lessened traffic on the Trace.

"
…the meals offered at stands consisted of only a mess of mush and milk, some fried bacon, and possibly some fresh meat
"

Archeology and Native Americans

*For more than a century the ghosts of a vanished nation
have ambuscaded in the vast solitudes of the continent,
and the forest-covered mounds have been usually regarded
as the mysterious sepulchers of its kings and nobles. It was
an alluring conjecture that a powerful people . . . once
occupied the valley.*

—J. W. Powell,
Bureau of American Ethnology, 1891

If you are fascinated by the power of ancient sites and
eager to know more about Native Americans of the Mississippi River valley, you will find the Parkway to be
chain of delights. The sites in Natchez and along the
roadway span 9,000 years, three ancient cultures, and
three modern tribes.

Prehistoric Sites
Of the seven mound locations within the Parkway
boundaries, all in Mississippi. Five are burial mounds
and two are ceremonial. Burial mounds are usually coni-
cal or rounded, and ceremonial mounds are generally
flat-topped to accommodate a religious structure, such
as a temple. Please don't walk on the mounds.

   The architects of the flat-top structures are called
Mississippian Mound Builders, referring not to the state
of Mississippi, but to the concentration of their
dwellings and villages in the Mississippi River Valley.
Although sometimes lacking precise links, historians
think that these people were the ancestors of the modern, or so-called historic tribes. Along the Parkway these
include the Natchez, the Choctaw, and the Chickasaw
nations, who all spoke Muskhogean languages. A tie has

"
*there are seven mound
locations within the
Parkway boundaries,
all in Mississippi,
five burial mounds and
two ceremonial*
"

been established between the Mound Builders of the breathtaking Emerald Mound and the Natchez tribe, who abandoned it and constructed Grand Village to be their ceremonial center. When the Spanish explorer de Soto marched through the area in 1540, the flat-top mounds were in use, but only the Natchez were still using them when the French arrived 160 years later. Internal strife, disease introduced by de Soto's men, and pressure from other tribes affected thousands of residents, and this probably caused the flat-top mounds to be largely abandoned by the Natchez.

Moving backward in time, several burial sites on the Parkway, including the Boyd, Bynum, and Pharr mounds, were inhabited by Woodland Period Indians. They developed a primitive agricultural society and made hunting more efficient, using the bow and arrow. They were also the first to domesticate corn.

Bear Creek Mound and the adjacent area, situated just below the Alabama state line, is one of the oldest occupied sites on the Parkway. This area was inhabited by humans, intermittently, for approximately 8,000 years, first by Paleo Indians from as early as BCE 7000, to Mississippian-era people around CE 1300. The Mississippians built this mound between CE 1200 and 1400 in several stages for ceremonial or elite residential use.

The Natchez

Until 1730, when it was obliterated by the French, the Natchez tribe was the historical link between the ancient and the modern-era Native American cultures. The Natchez had a closely-knit society that depended on agriculture, fishing, and hunting. Their tools were made of stone, wood, and bone until trade with white people gave them access to iron and steel. They lived around the area of the city of present-day Natchez, and their ceremonial mounds still stand at Grand Village.

Built upon eight- to ten-foot-high mounds, Natchez temples were rectangular, measured up to 20 by 40 feet, and oriented to the east. A bird effigy carved of wood rested upon the gabled roof ends. In a larger front room burned the eternal fire. The back of the building was a small, partitioned "holy room," where the stone idol or sacred stone was probably kept, and fine mats decorated the walls.

Although most daily rituals were similar to those of people everywhere, according to the NPS the Natchez had "the most spectacular, and at times the bloodiest religion of all the tribes north of Mexico." Their supreme deity was the sun. The high priest, called a Sun, was the earthly representative of the deity and was considered a descendent of it. The Sun wielded absolute power of life and death over his subjects. There were male and female Suns, with matriarchal lineage.

Funerals were exceptionally deadly affairs. The dead Sun's family and servants, and any friends and warriors who so desired, were strangled during the burial ceremony, as was an infant. Then the body of the Sun and his wife or wives were buried together in a trench inside the temple.

The Choctaw

The Choctaw tribe had the Southeast's best farmers, growing plenty of food to feed themselves with enough left over to barter. The tribe has only one surviving earth work. Their sacred mound of Nanih Waiya, located near present-day Noxapater, Mississippi (about 30 miles east of the Parkway near Kosciusko) is one of the more important surviving Native American sites in the state. It could be described as the "mecca" of Choctaw life and death. Like the Chickasaw, members of the Choctaw tribe still live in the greater Trace area.

Glimpses of Choctaw life along the Parkway emphasize tribal boundaries that moved several times to accommodate pioneer settlement. The 1820 Treaty of Doak's Stand was an important agreement between the U.S. government and the native peoples living in the Mississississippi–Alabama area. Negotiations between the white man and native peoples were set in writing in treaties, sometimes under the threat of coercion from government leaders, such as Andrew Jackson. You can also find evidence of the peaceful coexistence between the Choctaw and the new settlers in the stands, or inns they operated together, often as married couples. Pioneer mission schools point toward a more aggressive white imposition of the Old World culture on the area's native peoples.

The Chickasaw

A highly respected nation, the Chickasaw were by far the most warlike tribe in Mississippi. They fought as far north as the Great Lakes and as far south as the Gulf of Mexico. They sometimes fought alone; at times they allied with other Indian nations; and they had a perpetual partnership with the English. Ackia (pronounced "Hehkia"), near Tupelo, was the site of one of their most famous battles. Here, with some English aid, they defeated encroaching Choctaw and French forces. This definitive battle, on May 26, 1736, marked the beginning of the decline of the French presence west of the Appalachian Mountains.

Two stops along the Parkway address the coming together of the white and native peoples at U.S. government outposts for Indian relations known as "agencies:" the former site of an inn at Buzzard Roost Spring, and Monroe mission. At these sites you can learn about Chickasaw daily life, government, and dwellings. Tishomingo State Park, named for the last great warrior chief of the Chickasaw Nation, is particularly beautiful. Tishomingo died on the Trail of Tears in 1838 at age 102, and was buried near Little Rock. Tishomingo was "heart" of the tribe, and so he is represented on the Great Seal of the Chickasaw Nation.

Civil War and Other Military History

Gentle winds of Springtime seem a sighing over a thousand new-made graves.

—A Union soldier who
survived the Battle of Shiloh

In the way we think of uniformed soldiers, the first military presence along the Trace was that of de Soto and his men, although certainly Native Americans had organized fighting forces here long before de Soto's men arrived in 1540–1541. In 1801–1802 the U.S. Army stationed at the northern end of Garrison Creek to begin transforming the Old Trace into a more reliable road. In 1813 Andrew Jackson marched troops on the Trace for the War of 1812, and then in 1815 marched his men home again after defeating the British at the Battle of New Orleans. Two Civil War sites are located directly on the Parkway: the Battle of Raymond and the Confederate gravesites.

The area, however, has rich stories to tell about the Civil War era, and you may want to venture off the Parkway to visit Vicksburg, Tupelo, Brices Cross Roads, and Shiloh national memorials.

"We must this day conquer or perish!" were Albert Sidney Johnston's prophetic words on the morning of April 6, 1862 at Shiloh in Tennessee. By 2:30 that afternoon the Confederate commander was dead. This first major battle in the West, also known as Pittsburg Landing, was the bloodiest since the war began in 1861. After two days of fighting, nearly 24,000 men had been killed, wounded, or captured. This Confederate loss was the first in a chain of defeats, and by the evening of June 6, 1862, the western two-thirds of Tennessee was in Union hands.

Traveling to Vicksburg will make evident the Mississippi River's strategic importance in the Union's war efforts. The siege of Vicksburg, "The Gibraltar of the Confederacy," lasted from May 18 to July 4, 1863, subjecting the civilian population to regular shelling and deep deprivation. The loss of Vicksburg, along with Confederate failures at the Battle of Raymond and Port Gibson, inserted a fatal Union wedge into the Confederate States of America (CSA). When Port Hudson, Louisiana surrendered on July 8, 1863, the North gained complete control of the vital Mississippi River.

In a related but geographically separate effort, Union troops fought to cut through the Confederacy from northern Mississippi to the Atlantic Ocean at Savannah. You can learn more about this struggle, including the battles of Tupelo and Brices Cross Roads, by diverging off the Parkway. Both clashes involved the nearly mythic figure of CSA General Nathan Bedford Forrest. Commanding the cavalry he had outfitted at his own expense, Forrest was known as "That Devil Forrest" and "The Wizard of the Saddle" for his finesse and success. Forrest's goal was to interrupt the Union's ability to supply General William Tecumseh Sherman's infamous "March to the Sea."

While the battle of Brices Cross Roads, fought on June 10, 1864, was an overwhelming Confederate victory over a larger and better-equipped Union army, the battle at Tupelo on July 14–15, 1864 is regarded as either a Union victory or a draw. Both battles prevented Forrest from interrupting Sherman's railroad supply line through Louisville, Nashville, and Chattanooga. Both battlefield sites are commemorated by one-acre plots, and Brices Cross Roads has a museum.

Natural Wonders

A long park has replaced a wild forest.

—Paul R. Coppock,
in the *Memphis Commercial Appeal,*
December 26, 1976

In some ways the Parkway is one great outdoor museum, so it follows that many stops give you a chance to examine the Parkway's diverse natural features. Quite a few are simple, scenic picnic areas, while others have NPS interpretations that specifically address the surrounding flora and fauna. Almost all the nature walks are very short (under 10 to 15 minutes) and pretty easy to maneuver.

From Natchez, Mississippi to near Nashville, Tennessee the road cuts through six major forest types and eight major watersheds. The park ranges from 70 to 1100 feet in elevation, resulting in a variety of habitats.

Within the park, approximately 800 species of plants help to support more than 350 animal species, including a few that are quite rare. Look carefully and you may

"
in some ways the Parkway is one great outdoor museum
"

glimpse the Southern bald eagle, the red-cockaded woodpecker, and the gray bat—all endangered. The area's bayou darter, slackwater darter, and ringed saw-back turtle are also on the threatened list. Some of the more common wildlife along the entire length of the Parkway includes white-tailed deer, turkey, bobcat, raccoon, opossum, fox, coyote, and field- and forest-dwelling songbirds. (See Chapter Two, "The Nuts and Bolts of Traveling the Trace" (p. 29), for more information on potentially dangerous species you might encounter.)

Natchez, the southern terminus of the Natchez Trace Parkway, is located on a bluff 100 feet above the Mississippi River—definitely a sight worth seeing. From here the Parkway winds northeast through beech and oak forests, with some trees draped with Spanish moss. It enters the Southern Pine Hills near Raymond, Mississippi and passes through the Jackson Prairie, now occupied by the Jackson metropolitan area and the Ross Barnett Reservoir. From the northeastern tip of the reservoir, the Parkway crosses pine and dry-oak forests in Mississippi's North Central Hills, Flatwoods, and Pontotoc Ridge provinces. European settlers leased large parts of these woodland areas to plant cotton in the red clay soil. This gave rise to the region's antebellum society. The plantations have long since vanished, but agriculture remains important in this part of the state.

The alluvial agricultural soils around Tupelo are part of the Black Belt Prairie and were an important resource to the Chickasaw and the prehistoric Indians who preceded them. North of Tupelo, the Parkway cuts through a mixture of pine and hardwood forests in the hills above the Tombigbee River. The Parkway then makes its way up onto Alabama's Cumberland Plateau, the westernmost extension of the legendary Appalachian Mountain range.

The Parkway drops from the plateau into the Tennessee River Valley of northeastern Alabama with its red clay soils, excellent for growing cotton. It then traverses forests dominated primarily by oak and hickory on Tennessee's Highland Rim, where the road curves more as it reaches its highest elevation of 1,100 feet above sea level. The Parkway terminus at Pasquo, Tennessee, 15 miles outside of Nashville proper, is on the eastern edge of the Nashville Basin, an area similar to the bluegrass region of Kentucky.

The more fertile farmlands along the 444-mile-long

"

Natchez, located on a bluff 100 feet above the Mississippi River, is definitely a sight worth seeing

"

Parkway are devoted to the production of milo (a type of sorghum), soybeans, corn, wheat, and cotton, while marginal agricultural lands are used primarily for grazing cattle and horses.

The Living Trace

All life used this Trace, and he liked to see the animals move along it in direct, oblivious journey, for they had begun it and made it, the buffalo and deer and the small running creatures before man ever where he wanted to go . . .

—Eudora Welty, *A Still Moment*

The Living Trace category is a way to consider the lives of people who have lived and worked alongside the Trace.

It's virtually impossible to imagine all that has happened along this shifting route used by thousands of people over the years. Only now and again can we catch glimpses of their experiences, customs, and everyday routines.

Some were rich, such as those who built Windsor Ruins, but most others led more commonplace, sometimes hardscrabble, lives. The town of Rocky Springs, for example, thrived for decades, but now only a few relics remain: two safes that were probably too heavy to move, and a church that still gathers faithful in the area for regular services. Witch Dance still keeps alive a different kind of belief: where witches dance, the grass turns brown. French Camp began as a trading post, but early on became a school. It survives today as a stable rural community. At the Mississippi Crafts Center you'll find evidence of another constantly evolving Trace living legacy: the creativity and skill of people who have lived here for centuries and people who have only just arrived to the Trace environs.

Tennessee's Gordon house, and the more contemporary tobacco farm, are the structures of families whose primary sustenance came from the land itself. Unlike so many Trace travelers just passing through, these people attached themselves to the region because of what it had to offer: a chance to succeed in spite of inevitable change.

The major bridges listed below point to other kinds of changes—improvements that would make any

> **"**
>
> *Witch Dance still keeps alive a different kind of belief: where witches dance, the grass turns brown*
>
> **"**

ancient Trace foot- or horse-traveler howl with envy for the ease that the bridges' engineered spans provide.

The travelers made the Trace famous, but the stories told by these markers are just as vital and as much a part of the Trace story as you are.

21.0	**Springfield Plantation** (p. 79)	
30.0	**Windsor Ruins (heading north)** (p. 79)	
41.0	**Windsor Ruins (heading south)** (p. 81)	
54.8	**Rocky Springs** (p. 83)	
93.0	**Coles Mead Cemetery** (p. 87)	
102.4	**Mississippi Crafts Center** (p. 87)	
107.9	**West Florida Boundary** (p. 90)	
160.0	**Information Center** (p. 94)	
180.7	**French Camp** (p. 95)	
233.2	**Witch Dance** (p. 99)	
293.2	**Tennessee–Tombigbee Waterway and Jamie L. Whitten Bridge** (p. 110)	
328.6–327.8	**John Coffee Memorial Bridge** (p. 116)	
381.8	**Napier Mine** (p. 120)	
401.4	**Tobacco Farm** (p. 125)	
407.7	**Gordon House** (p. 127)	
438.0	**Highway 96 Double-Arch Bridge** (p. 130)	

National Park Service (NPS) Information

For more than two decades it was the most significant highway of the Old Southwest and one of the most important in the nation. It was an avenue of exploration, international rivalry, warfare, trade, settlement, and development. This old road . . . recalls an early and heroic chapter in our national epic.

—Dawson Phelps, *An Administrative History of the Natchez Trace Parkway*

For help in sorting out the many stories of the Old Trace, the Tupelo Visitor Center—which is also the Parkway's administrative headquarters—is a must. Located near the midpoint of the Parkway, this stop has the most complete interpretive overview of the Trace's history and touring options. It also has Trace-related books, music, and gifts for sale, as well as rest rooms, and a knowledgeable, dedicated staff. The Tupelo Visitor Center is open from 8 a.m. to 5 p.m. year-round except on Christmas Day.

The campground ranger stations at Rocky Springs, Jeff Busby, and Meriwether Lewis are also good sources of information. The campsites are free, so there is not a regularly staffed gatehouse, and thus you may have to hunt for a ranger. Although Mount Locust is not a campground, it is regularly staffed both at the historic house and at the small office down the hill to the right as you face the old farmhouse and inn.

Due to federal NPS budget cuts, it is very hard to catch somebody "at home" at the Dancy and Colbert Ferry ranger stations. This is particularly frustrating when, as at the Colbert Ferry office, you can see interpretive exhibits and information within the locked glass enclosure. If you love our national parks, lobby for their support!

15.5	Mount Locust Ranger Station (p. 77)
54.8	Rocky Springs Ranger Station (p. 83)
193.1	Jeff Busby Ranger Station (p. 96)
214.5	Dancy Ranger Station (p. 98)
266.0	Tupelo Visitor Center (Parkway Headquarters) (p. 106)
327.3	Colbert Ferry Ranger Station (p. 116)
385.9	Meriwether Lewis Ranger Station (p. 121)

All stations except Dancy have rest rooms and water fountains.

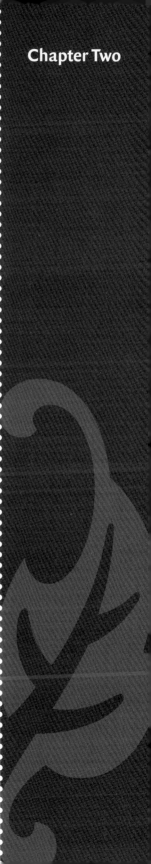

Chapter Two

The Nuts and Bolts of Traveling the Trace

● ●

*Surrounded on each side with a deep wall of woods, I
enjoyed the serenity of the evening in silent meditation:
everything I saw and heard taught me a lesson which
required not the powers of oratory to embellish it.*

—Francis Bailey, Trace traveler in 1797

HOW TO USE THE MILEPOSTS

The Trace is a wonderful way to loosen yourself from
everyday constraints as its rhythms lull you into imagin-
ing the many activities that have occurred here over
thousands of years. Every so often, though, it helps to
know where you are on the 444-mile stretch.

Each mile of the Trace is marked on the right-hand
side (heading north) or on the left-hand side (heading
south) by unobtrusive, simple posts with a yellow
engraved number. The miles run from south to north,
just as they would've been experienced by the thousands
of Kaintucks, the boatmen from the mid-South and
above, who walked or rode a horse north on the Trace
toward home.

The mileposts can help you calculate how far you have to go until the next crossroad or until the next place to stop and see something special along the Trace. They correspond to the Milepost Gazetteer on the Natchez Trace Parkway National Park Service maps, as well as to the milepost stops in this guide.

PARKWAY RULES

- ▲ Hunting and the possession of loaded firearms are prohibited.
- ▲ Nonrecreational hauling and commercial trucking are not allowed.
- ▲ Tent and trailer camping are permitted only at designated campgrounds.
- ▲ All natural, historical, and archeological objects are protected by federal law.
- ▲ Build fires only in fire rings and grills.
- ▲ The Natchez Trace Parkway is a designated bike route; watch for bikers and yield when necessary.
- ▲ All Terrain Vehicles (ATVs) are prohibited on the Parkway.
- ▲ Report all accidents, fires, and emergencies to the nearest park ranger.

EMERGENCIES

If an emergency arises while you are on the Parkway, call (800) 300-PARK (7275).

A LITTER-FREE TRACE

Please make life easier for the Parkway's outstanding maintenance staff and use the garbage cans located at every stop.

SPEEDING ALONG ON THE PARKWAY

The speed limits on the Natchez Trace Parkway, generally 50 miles per hour or slower, are enforced and should be heeded. The rewards of obeying the speed limits are several.

The point of traveling the Trace is to enjoy the scenery, and slowing down from the usual 70-plus miles per hour on the interstate makes a measurable difference in your ability to take in all that the countryside has to offer.

Potential traffic hazards on the Trace include a number of people on motorcycles and bicycles, as well as wildlife, especially deer. A slower pace helps you notice these and react in a timely manner.

The Trace is well monitored by Parkway rangers, and more than one local will tell you that they *will* ticket you for speeding. Do not be deceived into thinking that no patrol cars are on duty if you have not seen them. They can be two minutes ahead or behind you, and they also monitor your speed using a radar. The occasional speeding car will pass you, but do not take up that faster traffic tempo, for odds are great that you will be caught and fined.

TIMING YOUR TRIP

In 2003 the Parkway logged more than 5 million recreational visits to its roughly 52,000 total acres. Most visitors travel in the fall and spring, but the Trace never feels crowded. It is possible, in fact, to see only ten cars in 30 miles on a gorgeous spring day.

The Trace parallels Colbert Creek at Rock Spring (at milepost 330.2)

As for daily timing, make sure you reach the Tupelo Visitor Center headquarters between the hours of 8 a.m. and 5 p.m, and expect to spend at least half an hour there.

WEATHER AND CLIMATE

Spring and fall attract visitors when the weather is more temperate. Winter is usually cold and damp with occasional warm periods. Summer tends to be very hot and humid, even more so the closer you get to Natchez.

For travelers a century ago weather was the greatest obstacle to comfortable travel. Dr. Rush Nutt, a Trace survivor, stated in his diary, "Rains annually commence in January and February which causes all the creeks to overflow the lowlands, and continue high until March or April, during which time the traveler meets with considerable difficulty in passing them."

In wet weather, the swamps at various points along the Trace were almost impassable and constituted one of the greatest hazards of Old Trace travel. In especially wet periods, some portions of the Parkway can still become impassable due to water.

Long-gone Trace traveler Adam Hodgson wrote of plunging in some swamps "up to the saddle-skirts in mire at every step. The bottom is stiff clay, and horses sometimes stick so fast that they cannot be extricated, but are left to die."

Tornadoes could make the Trace an indiscernible, impervious thicket, and Learner Blackman was one of those few who experienced a snowstorm while traveling the Trace long ago. "I was as near frozen as I ever was in my life," he wrote. "The snow became near a foot deep, and the Trace having been softened by a recent rain, we could not walk to warm ourselves and had to sit on our horses and bear the cold as best we could."

Let us count our present-day creature-comfort blessings, but do roll down the windows and breathe in the benefits of the Parkway as befits the season.

WHAT TO WEAR

Of course, vacation enjoyment dictates comfortable clothing, and the key here is footwear. Closed-toe shoes are highly recommended if you want to do any walking. Although the many short nature trails are generally well kept, some have long grasses, so sturdy shoes are best, particularly for sections of the Old Trace.

"

for travelers a century ago weather was the greatest obstacle to comfortable travel

"

HOW SAFE IS THE TRACE?

Good sense is always a critical ingredient for safe travel, but you need not fear bandits and murderers the way the Old Trace travelers did. It is not a good idea to leave your car unlocked if you are out of its sight, but this is a normal precaution under almost all circumstances.

Keep aware, but don't let the remote possibility of danger deprive you of doing what you want to do. The Parkway has a low crime rate, probably due in good measure to the constant patrol of Parkway rangers and police.

NATURAL DANGERS

Much more likely than an encounter with a mugger is a run-in with **poison ivy** (*Toxicodendron radicans*), which is found all over the Trace. It can appear as a tree-climbing hairy vine, a ground cover trailing vine, or more rarely as a low shrub. The rubric "Leaves of three, let it be" is a good guide. You can be affected by poison ivy in every season, and, in fact, the plant is particularly virulent in the late winter and early spring, when it resembles just another twig jutting out of the ground. The best way to prevent a reaction is to prevent contact by wearing closed-toe shoes, long pants, and long sleeves. Don't let your dog rummage through poison ivy either, as you can contract a reaction from an animal's fur. If you know you have been exposed, attend to the area right away. Clean the exposed skin with rubbing alcohol if you can. Next, wash the skin with cold water but do not scrub. Finally, take a shower with regular soap and water. A bath should be avoided, as it will only circulate the allergen all over your body. Tecnu Outdoor Skin Cleanser, specifically formulated to break down urushiol, is great travel product that's available at many drug stores. It works well.

Chiggers are the larva of *Trombicula*, known in their adult stages as harvest mites. They are almost impossible to see with the naked eye, but are reddish-orange. Chiggers are fast and quickly latch

Poison Ivy

on to your legs or feet. They then search for a confined place, such as ankles, behind knees, armpits, or groins. Brushing your body and clothes with a towel will help to knock them off. At your first opportunity take a shower and scrub well. Over-the-counter antihistamines will help with any you missed. Chigger bites won't hurt you, but they can drive you crazy with their itch.

The Trace area has two species of **ticks.** If you should find a lone star tick (*Amblyomma americanum*) or wood

tick (*Dermancentor andersonii*) on your body, remove it by grasping it just behind the point of attachment with tweezers or, holding tissue or cloth, use your fingers. Pull straight out using steady pressure. Wash the bite area and apply antiseptic. Tick-borne dis-

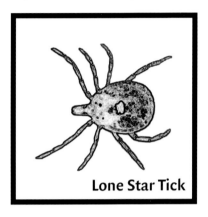

Lone Star Tick

eases such as Rocky Mountain Spotted Fever and Erlichosis are a possibility, so watch for abnormal health symptoms.

Venomous snakes are another potential danger of which you should be aware along the Trace. Tiber rattlesnakes (*Crotalus horridus*); Eastern diamondback rattlesnakes (*Crotalus adamanteus*); pygmy rattlesnakes (*Sistrurus miliarius*); copperheads (*Agkistrodon contortrix mokasen*) and cottonmouths (*Agkistrodon piscivorus piscivorus*), a type of water snake;

are all found in along the Trace. This is a daunting species list, but you are not likely to encounter any of them, and they will only bite if they are surprised, cornered, or threatened.

To avoid snakes along the Park-

Rattlesnake

way's trails, watch carefully where you put your feet. Camoflage is a snake's great ally, and the leafy forest floor is a logical place to stumble upon them. When you step over logs be especially mindful that a snake is not snoozing on the far side. Making noise in the woods as you go your way is a good idea, as it lets all the wild ones give you a wide berth. Any snake can bite you and every wound should be attended to immediately.

No matter what the species, please don't take it upon yourself to kill with your car snakes sunning in the roadway. They pose you no threat, and the precious little remaining wild is the only place they have to live.

White-tailed deer (*Odocoileus virginianus*) are numerous along the Parkway and frequently cross the roadway at inopportune times. Always be on the lookout for them, especially at twilight. If you see one cross the road, watch and wait for more to follow—they are herd animals. Late fall is an especially precarious time as mating season provokes more movement. Even when you're driving at or under the 50-mph speed limit, a collision with a deer can be very dangerous for all involved.

For much more in-depth information on critters consult *Dangerous Wildlife of the Southeast: A Guide to Safe Encounters at Home and in the Wild,* written by your friendly author of this book, F. Lynne Bachleda. *The Dangerous Wildlife Series,* published by Menasha Ridge Press, also has volumes on California and Nevada, the Mid-Atlantic, and the Southwest.

CHILDREN'S ACTIVITIES

Pioneer Days provide an opportunity for kids to learn leatherworking, basket making, and other pioneer crafts firsthand from living history demonstrators. Pioneer Days typically occur at the Parkway Visitor Center, near Tupelo, Mississippi (milepost 266) about ten Saturdays each year. Check out the News & Events section on the park's Web site, **www.nps.gov/natr,** or call (800) 305-7417.

The Natchez Trace Parkway newspaper, *The Trace Traveler,* has Junior Ranger activities to be completed by students and children in order to earn a Junior Ranger badge. Notification of complete Junior Ranger activities can be mailed to the Superintendent, 2680 Natchez Trace Parkway, Tupelo, MS 38804 to receive your badge. The activities include a brief history of the Natchez Trace Parkway, Old Trace history, boatmen's travels, a word

"

making noise in the woods as you go your way is a good idea, as it lets all the wild ones give you a wide berth

"

search, "litter" known facts, a naturalist's notebook, and other activities focusing on preservation and history.

GAS, FOOD, AND LODGING

One of the great surprises of being on the Parkway is how far away you can feel from civilization, and yet how close it is. Numerous crossroads connect you with nearby places to get gas, buy food, and find a room for the night.

Gasoline

There is only one place to buy gasoline on the Parkway itself. That is at **Jeff Busby,** which is also a campground and ranger station, at milepost 193.1, roughly midway between the beginning and end of the Parkway.

Food

The gas station at Jeff Busby has a small market that has the usual road-food snacks. In general you will need to leave the Parkway to find vittles. A better option is to take a cooler and picnic along the way.

There are many chain restaurants in the towns adjacent to the Parkway, especially Tupelo and Jackson. Consult the Chamber of Commerce listings in the Appendixes (p. 146) for specifics on independent options. There are also a few special spots where good food and great atmosphere will make your trip more memorable.

In Natchez you can eat at the **King's Tavern,** built prior to 1789 and purported to be "the oldest building in the Natchez Territory." In the early Trace heydays this was the end of the journey for post riders. The combination tavern and post office was a local hangout for Natchez residents and weary travelers until 1820. For protection against outlaws, this was a good place for folks to meet and form groups to walk the Trace together. Of course, the outlaws frequented King's Tavern, too.

Used next by the Postlehwaite family as a residence for nearly 150 years, King's Tavern was then purchased and restored by the Pilgrimage Garden Club in 1970. Today King's Tavern still caters to Parkway adventurers and natives by offering cocktails, prime rib, steaks, seafood, and pasta. The building is steeped in history, mystery, and good stories. A jeweled Spanish dagger came to light when a chimney collapsed in early 1900; three skeletons were unearthed from the ground floor in 1930; and reports of ghosts are numerous. Ask the wait staff and read the back of the wine list card for more information.

"
... eat at the King's Tavern, built prior to 1789, and purported to be 'the oldest building in the Natchez Territory'
"

King's Tavern, 619 Jefferson Street (at the intersection with Rankin), Natchez, MS 39120; phone (601) 446-8878 for reservations which are not essential but always a good idea. Daily, 5 p.m.–10 p.m. Entrées start at $10.

Also in Natchez, have lunch at the **Carriage House Restaurant** on the grounds of Stanton Hall. This not-to-be-missed antebellum mansion is now the headquarters for the Pilgrimage Garden Club. (For more information on Stanton Hall and the Spring and Fall Pilgrimages please see sidebar "The Millionaires of Natchez" on page 68.) Nationally famous, the venue serves a full menu of tasty Southern cooking including fried chicken, baked ham with raisin sauce, gumbo, homemade salads, and desserts. The biscuits will slay you, and you can enjoy mint juleps in the King's Lounge.

Hostesses dressed in Antebellum style greet guests at a mansion in Natchez

The Carriage House Restaurant, 401 High Street, Natchez, MS 39120; phone (601) 445-5151; ***www.discover ourtown.com/webs/natchezms/carriagehouse.*** *Lunch, 11 a.m.–2:30 p.m. daily; open for dinner only during Pilgrimages. Expect to pay approximately $10 for a full lunch.*

If you make the excursion to see Windsor Ruins, you will wind up in Port Gibson. Just before you come to the main drag in Port Gibson, MS 61, on your right you will pass the **Restoration Café,** housed in an old, airy building constructed in 1839. Here you can choose from soups, interesting salads, sandwiches served on homemade bread (or herbed wraps if you prefer), and daily entrée specials. Flavored coffees, herbal tees, and baked items are also available.

Restoration Café, 212 Carrol Street, Port Gibson, MS 39150; phone (601) 437-3186. Monday–Friday, 8 a.m.–3 p.m.; $2–$7 and possibly more for entrées.

There is one restaurant right along the Parkway at French Camp milepost 180.7. The **Council House Café,** a ministry of French Camp Academy, is a wonderful place to stop for healthy portions of sandwiches, soups, and broccoli salad. All sandwiches are made with fresh homemade bread, and there's fresh Mississippi mud cake and bread pudding for dessert. You can eat inside an historic log cabin or sit on the porch.

A small bridge spans the Natchez Trace Parkway

*Council House Café, French Camp at milepost 180.7. Phone (662) 547-9860; **www.frenchcamp.org/council house.html**. Monday–Saturday, 10:30 a.m.–2:30 p.m., $2–$6.*

Tupelo has many places to eat. Stop in at the Parkway Visitor Center daily between 8 a.m. and 5 p.m. to get recommendations and directions.

David Crockett State Park just west of Lawrenceburg, Tennessee has a restaurant. The food at Tennessee's state parks buffets is notoriously good, and they offer a copious supply of famous Southern cuisine.

David Crockett State Park Restaurant, exit at milepost 370 and head east on TN 64 toward Lawrenceburg. Breakfast, Saturday–Sunday, 7:30 a.m.–10 a.m., $5.50 plus drink. Lunch, Sunday–Thursday, 11 a.m.–2 p.m., $7.25. Dinner, Friday–Saturday, 4:30 p.m.–7:30 p.m., $10.45.

At the northern terminus of the Parkway you can partake of what's been a Nashville tradition since 1951 by eating at the **Loveless Café.** You can see it from the Parkway as you exit on TN 100 going east toward Nashville. Recently renovated by homeboy and caterer-to-the-stars Tom Morales, the Loveless starts serving their famous breakfasts at 6 a.m. during the week and at 7 a.m. on the weekends. Biscuits, renowned country ham, stone-ground grits, and strong drinks are just a few of the offerings. The breakfast items are so sought after, the staff continues serving them until 5 p.m. Lunch is a choice of down-home favorites like fried chicken, catfish, and chicken livers or gizzards. There are salads, soups, sandwich plates, and kid's plates. Dinner starts at 5 p.m. and tosses into the mix chicken and dumplings, beef tenderloin, trout, and smoked pork chops. Sides are too numerous to list. Pies, cobblers, made-from-scratch banana pudding, brownies, and vanilla ice cream will finish you off, if the drinks haven't already accomplished that.

Don't be fooled by the "motel" in the name. The old motel's rooms have been converted into other businesses, including Hams and Jams, where you can have the Loveless wonders shipped "anywhere," and you can get a basket of goodies together for a picnic along the Parkway. There's also a bike shop and a canoe and kayak outfitter, both of whom will rent you equipment. Jewelry, art, and gifts add other offerings.

*Loveless Café and Motel, 8400 Highway 100, Nashville, TN 37221. Phone (615) 646-9700; **www.lovelesscafe.com**. Breakfast, 6 a.m.–5 p.m. weekdays; weekend breakfast starts*

"

partake of what's been a Nashville tradition since 1951 by eating at the Loveless Café

"

at 7 a.m. Lunch, 11 a.m.–5 p.m. daily. Dinner, 5 p.m.–9 p.m. Breakfast à la carte items start at $1.50; breakfast plates and platters, $6–$10; lunch items, $3–$10; dinner entrées, $9–$19.

Lodging

For indoor accommodations, consult the Appendixes (p. 141) for nearby motels and hotels. You can also call (800) 377-2770 for bed-and-breakfast options. If you prefer to be closer to nature, read on.

Camping along the Natchez Trace

There are several options for camping along the Parkway. In the Appendixes (p. 151), you will find a complete list provided by the NPS that includes privately run facilities. It's always a good idea to call and confirm about specific features and programs to make sure they are available.

National Park Service Campgrounds

There are three federal campgrounds directly on the Parkway:

▲ Rocky Springs

▲ Jeff Busby

▲ Meriwether Lewis

There are no fees for their use. Individual sites have tables, grills, and a level tent site. Rest rooms and drinking water are provided, but no hot water, showers, electrical or sanitary hookups, or dumping sites are available. Stays are a maximum of 15 days during periods of heavy visitation. Campgrounds are open year-round, with peak seasons of use being spring and fall.

Rules and policies for federal campgrounds along the Parkway:

▲ Campsites are first come, first served, and therefore cannot be reserved.

▲ All campsites are free.

▲ Camp and park only at sites.

▲ Hours of quiet are from 10 p.m. to 6 a.m.

▲ Do not disturb the ground.

▲ Please leave a clean campsite.

▲ Build fires only in fireplaces; burn only dead or downed wood; observe campfire restrictions.

▲ Pets must be leashed at all times (physically restrained).

▲ Fireworks and firearms are prohibited.

▲ Organized groups should contact the Superintendent at (800) 305-7417.

Rocky Springs Site (milepost 54.8)

In the 1790s new settlers were attracted to this area by the rich soil and multiple fresh-water springs. They cleared the land, constructed homes, and, in 1837, built an impressive brick church still used for worship. By 1860 Rocky Springs was a prosperous rural community of more than 2,000 people. But between 1860 and 1920 the area was devastated by the Civil War, yellow fever, the boll weevil, and land erosion. Today only the church and cemetery, two rusting safes, and abandoned cisterns mark the site. The Rocky Springs facility includes the 22-site campground, picnic tables, horseback riding, phone, self-guided trails through the town site and to the spring, and a hiking trail on the Old Trace. Camping and picnicking supplies are available at Port Gibson or Utica, both about 15 miles away.

Jeff Busby Site (milepost 193.1)

This campground is named for Thomas Jefferson Busby, the U.S. Congressman from Mississippi who introduced a bill that resulted in the 1934 act authorizing a survey of the Old Natchez Trace. On May 18, 1938 the Natchez Trace Parkway was authorized as a unit of the National Park System. From here you can walk to Little Mountain, one of Mississippi's highest points on the Parkway at 603 feet above sea level. Jeff Busby includes the 18-site campground, picnic tables, exhibit shelter and overlook atop Little Mountain, phone, and trails. A concessionaire operates the service station and camp store.

"

new settlers were attracted to this area by the rich soil and multiple fresh-water springs. They cleared the land, constructed homes, and, in 1837, built an impressive brick church still used for worship

"

Meriwether Lewis Site (milepost 385.9)

In 1809 at Grinder's Inn Meriwether Lewis, co-captain of the Lewis and Clark expedition and one-time governor of the Upper Louisiana Territory, died of gunshot wounds. A monument, designed as a broken shaft, marks his grave. The facilities include a 32-site campground, pioneer cemetery, picnic tables, ranger station, exhibits, phone, rest rooms, and trails. Camping and picnicking supplies and gasoline are available west of the parkway on TN 20 in Hohenwald.

Mississippi State Parks within 15 Miles of the Parkway

To receive literature on the parks listed below call (800) GO-PARKS (467-2757) or (601) 432-2222. Mississippi

State Parks charge a day-use fee of $2 per car plus $0.50 per person over four people. Pedestrians and bicycles are charged $0.50 per person. Motorcycles are $2 per person. Charges for specific activities may apply. A Mississippi fishing license is required for all persons between the ages of 16 and 65 and may be purchased at the park office for a nominal fee. Camping fees are $9–$15 per night.

Natchez State Park
230-B Wickliff Road
Natchez, Mississippi 39120
(601) 442-2658
Exit near milepost 8, 10 miles north of Natchez off US 61 at Stanton, Mississippi

Located 10 miles north of historic Natchez, this is the oldest settlement on the Mississippi River. Prior to the Civil War, more than half of the millionaires in the United States lived in Natchez and constructed elegant mansions unrivaled in size and elegance by any in the nation. Most of these splendid homes were spared during the Civil War, and many are now open for tours.

Number of campsites 50 for RVs

Each site has Picnic table, grill, electrical and water hook-ups; 6 sites have sewage hook-ups

Cabins 10 lakeside, air-conditioned cabins with bed and bath linens, and basic kitchen equipment

Facilities Sewage dump station, rest rooms, hot showers

Reservations Strongly recommended

Pets Not allowed in cabins

Other Natchez Lake stocked for fishing; no extra charge. Picnic area a half mile from lake, with 10 tables and grills; pavilion available for rental

Trace State Park
2139 Faulkner Road
Belden, MS 38826
(662) 489-2958
tracesp@ayrix.net
Exit at milepost 260 on MS 6 West

Trace State Park is a quiet, natural retreat located 9 miles west of Tupelo, one of Mississippi's fastest-growing cities. It offers a variety of outdoor activities, from fishing and water sports to hiking on miles of secluded nature trails. A special arrangement with the Pontotoc

"
prior to the Civil War, more than half of the millionaires in the United States lived in Natchez and constructed elegant mansions unrivaled in size and elegance by any in the nation
"

Country Club allows Trace State Park guests to enjoy the club's 18-hole golf course without paying green fees.

Number of campsites 10 for developed tent camping; 8 primitive sites; 52 for RVs

RV sites have Picnic table, grill, electrical and water hook-ups; 6 sites have sewage hook-ups

Cabins 6 air-conditioned cabins with bed and bath linens, and basic kitchen equipment; outdoor grills; porches overlooking Trace Lake

Facilities Sewage dump station, rest rooms, hot showers in developed camping area; picnic tables and bathhouse near primitive camping area

Reservations A limited number of sites are set aside for advance reservations; the rest are first come, first served

Other Natchez Lake stocked for fishing, available for water sports; boat rentals and access to boat ramps; 25 picnic sites throughout park with tables and grills; 25 miles of trails for use by ATVs, motorcycles (helmets required), horses, and mountain bikes

Tombigbee State Park
264 Cabin Drive
Tupelo, MS 38804
(662) 842-7669
Exit at milepost 260 on MS 6 East

Located just 6 miles south of Tupelo, Tombigbee State Park offers outdoor recreation opportunities minutes from Tupelo. A scenic ridge overlooking Lake Lee provides the ideal spot for tent camping.

Number of campsites 20 for RV camping; primitive camping area with 2 picnic tables, 2 grills

RV sites have Picnic table, grill, electrical and water hook-ups

Cabins 7 air-conditioned cabins (2–6 people) with bed and bath linens, a fireplace, and basic kitchen equipment; a screened porch or a patio

Facilities Sewage dump station, rest rooms, hot showers in developed camping area; picnic tables and bathhouse near primitive camping area

Reservations Strongly recommended

Pets Not allowed in cabins

Other Lake Lee stocked for fishing (free with license), available for water sports; fishing and paddleboat rentals;

2 lakeside picnic sites throughout park with tables and grills; two picnic pavilions; 18-hole disc golf course; 3 nature trails.

Tishomingo State Park

P.O. Box 880
Tishomingo, Mississippi 38873
(662) 438-6914
Exit at milepost 304 to MS 25

Located in the foothills of the Appalachian Mountains, Tishomingo State Park is steeped in history and scenic beauty. Archeological excavations confirm the presence of Paleo Indians in the area now encompassed by the park as early as BCE 7000. The park takes its name from the leader of the Chickasaw nation, Chief Tishomingo. The Natchez Trace Parkway runs directly through the park. Today's visitors to Tishomingo State Park discover the same timeless natural beauty that enchanted the Indians centuries ago. Tishomingo offers a unique landscape of massive rock formations and fern-filled crevices found nowhere else in Mississippi. Massive boulders blanketed in moss dot the hillsides, and colorful wildflowers border trails once walked by Native Americans.

> *massive boulders blanketed in moss dot the hillsides, and colorful wildflowers border trails once walked by Native Americans*

Number of campsites 62 for RV camping; primitive camping area with water, rest rooms, and showers

RV sites have Picnic table, grill, electrical and water hook-ups; each RV pad offers direct access to Haynes Lake

Cabins 6 rustic air-conditioned cabins (4–6 people) with bed and bath linens, basic kitchen equipment, heat, a screened porch or a patio, and fireplace

Facilities Sewage dump station, rest rooms, hot showers in developed camping area; picnic tables and bathhouse near primitive camping area

Reservations A limited number of campsites are set aside for advance reservations; the rest are first come, first served; cabin reservations strongly recommended

Pets Not allowed in cabins

Other Haynes Lake stocked for fishing (free with license); fishing-boat rentals; swimming pool with shower facilities; float trips down Bear Creek; 50 picnic sites throughout park with tables and grills; 3 picnic pavilions with electricity; 13-mile trail system; nature center; swinging bridge; 18-hole disc golf course; rock climbing

Tennessee State Parks within 15 Miles of the Parkway

To receive literature on the park listed below, call (888) TN-PARKS (867-2757). Camping fees are $14–$18 per day.

David Crockett State Park

1400 West Gaines
Lawrenceburg, TN 38464-0398
(931) 762-9408 (office)
(931) 762-9541 (restaurant)
Exit milepost 370 on US 64 East

David Crockett—pioneer, soldier, politician, and industrialist—was born near the little town of Limestone in northeast Tennessee in 1786. In 1817, he moved to Lawrence County and served as a justice of the peace, a colonel of the militia, and as a state representative. Along the banks of Shoal Creek, in what is now his namesake park, Crockett established a diversified industry consisting of a powder mill, a gristmill, and a distillery. All three operations were washed away in a flood in September 1821. Financial difficulties from this loss

A monument marking
the grave of explorer
Meriwether Lewis
(at milepost 385.9)

caused Crockett to move to West Tennessee, where he was elected to Congress. While in Washington, he fought for his people's right to keep the land on which they had settled on the new frontier of West Tennessee. Crockett died at the Alamo Mission in March 1836 while aiding the Texans in their fight for independence from Mexico. Dedicated in May 1959 in honor of one of Tennessee's most famous native sons, David Crockett State Park is a half-mile west of Lawrenceburg.

Number of campsites 2 campgrounds, 107 sites total, with water, rest rooms, and showers

Sites have Picnic table, grill, electrical and water hook-ups; each RV pad offers direct access to Haynes Lake

Cabins 6 rustic air-conditioned cabins (4–6 people) with bed and bath linens, basic kitchen equipment, heat, a screened porch or a patio, and fireplace

Facilities Sewage dump station, rest rooms, hot showers

Reservations First come, first served; 2-week stay limit; cabin reservations strongly recommended

Pets Not allowed in cabins

Other Lindsey Lake stocked for fishing (license required); row- and pedal-boat rentals; swimming pool with shower facilities and concessions; restaurant; bicycle trail; hiking trails; tennis, softball, volleyball, and table-tennis facilities

"

David Crockett died at the Alamo Mission in March 1836 while aiding the Texans in their fight for independence from Mexico

"

Chapter Three

The Many Ways to Travel the Trace

• •

*The Mississippi River remains what it always was, the
Nile of the Western Hemisphere.*

—author John Gunther

It was the pull and power of the Mississippi River that
made the Trace famous, and now the Parkway has a
power of its own. There are many ways to experience
today's Natchez Trace.

MOTORIZED VEHICLES

This is the most common way folks travel the Parkway
today. Non-recreational commercial hauling is prohibited,
but you will see cars hauling camping trailers, as well as
trucks pulling horse trailers. RVs are quite common, too,
enjoying the more modest speed of 50 miles per hour. RV
drivers and those pulling large camping trailers should
take heed—a few pull-offs and sections of the Old Trace
will not accommodate turn-arounds or safe passage.

In some ways it seems the Parkway was made for
motorcycles. The open, incredibly scenic roadway sum-
mons riders of all ages in what can be a roaring, romantic
way to spend an afternoon.

Add bicycles to the mix, and you've got pretty much a full house for accidents, so take care not to get so lost in the scenery in front of you that you lose track of what's near you on the road.

BICYCLES

Touring bikes are another common sight on the Parkway. The section nearest Nashville is hilly and curving, but much of the Parkway is generally flatter and more of a straightaway. The general atmosphere here, especially with the absence of trucks, is that of a sunny country back road.

The premier sourcebook for those who wish to bicycle on the Parkway—and a wise investment of $15.95—is Glen Wanner's *Bicycling the Natchez Trace: A Guide to the Natchez Trace Parkway and Nearby Scenic Routes.*

The National Park Service (phone (800) 305-7417 or (601) 680-4025) offers a packet of materials to assist bicyclists on the Trace.

Bicycling has become an increasingly popular activity on the Natchez Trace Parkway. To ensure a safe and enjoyable trip, bicyclists are encouraged not to use the following area during heavy traffic periods: Tupelo, Mississippi, mileposts 258–268, 7–8:30 a.m. and 3–5 p.m. on weekdays.

Stanton Hall, one of Natchez's most stately historical manors, is home to the Pilgrimage Garden Club

If you are planning an organized or group ride, a special-use permit is required. Contact the Chief Ranger's Office at (601) 680-4014, Monday through Friday, to obtain a permit and special information.

Although bicycling is permitted with the flow of traffic on the Parkway, extreme caution is advised on sections of the parkway with heavy vehicular traffic, such as in Tupelo, Mississippi. The width of the parkway varies with a wider right-of-way at areas of historical, scientific, and recreational value. All lands outside of this boundary, with the exception of Tishomingo State Park and Tombigbee National Forest in northeast Mississippi, are privately owned and require owner permission to use for any purpose.

Safe bicycling rules for the Natchez Trace Parkway:

- ▲ Observe all traffic regulations.
- ▲ Keep to the right and ride in a straight line. Always ride single file.
- ▲ Never hitch onto other vehicles or race in traffic.
- ▲ Never carry other riders or items that obstruct vision or prevent proper control of the bicycle.
- ▲ Be sure your bicycle is in perfect running condition, and your brakes operate efficiently.
- ▲ Wear a helmet and reflective clothing.
- ▲ Each bicycle must exhibit a white light on the front and a red light or red reflector on the rear during periods of low visibility or during the period between sundown and sunup.
- ▲ Always carry drinking water.
- ▲ Use proper hand signals for turning and stopping.
- ▲ Plan to be off the parkway by sundown.
- ▲ In case of emergency call (800) 300-PARK (7275).

Drinking water is available at the following mileposts:

15.5	Mount Locust
17.5	Coles Creek
54.8	Rocky Springs
102.4	Mississippi Crafts Center
122.6	River Bend
154.3	Holly Hill
159.8	Kosciusko Welcome Center
180.7	French Camp
193.1	Jeff Busby

233.2	Witch Dance
266.0	Tupelo Visitor Center
286.7	Pharr Mounds
327.3	Colbert Ferry
364.5	Lower Glenrock Branch
377.8	Jack's Branch`
385.9	Meriwether Lewis
404.7	Jackson Falls
407.7	Gordon House
427.6	Leipers' Fork

Bicycle Services Near the Parkway

Note: Some may offer rental bikes. No known services in Alabama.

Mississippi

Natchez

Western Auto Associate Store—Downtown
180 Sergeant South Prentiss Drive
Natchez, MS 39120
(601) 445-4186
Monday–Saturday, 8 a.m.–6 p.m.

Jackson area

The Bike Rack
2282 Lakeland Drive
Flowood, MS 39208
(601) 936-2100
Monday–Saturday, 10 a.m.–6 p.m.
www.thebikerackms.com

Indian Cycle Fitness & Outdoor
677 South Pear Orchard Road
Ridgeland, MS 39157
(601) 956-8383
Monday–Saturday, 10 a.m.–6 p.m.
www.indiancyclefitness.com

Tupelo

Bicycle Pacelines
2120 West Jackson Street
Tupelo, MS 38801
(601) 844-8660
Monday–Friday, 11 a.m.–6 p.m.;
Saturday, 10 a.m.–5 p.m.

The double-arch bridge spans a valley at Highway 96 in Tennessee (milepost 438.0)

Tennessee

Columbia

The Wheel
11 Public Square
Columbia, TN 38401
(615) 381-3225
Monday–Friday, 10 a.m.–6 p.m.; Saturday, 9 a.m.–3 p.m.

Franklin

Franklin Bicycle Co.
124 Watson Glen
Franklin, TN 37064
(615) 790-2702
Monday–Saturday, 10 a.m.–6 p.m.; summer Sundays, 1–5 p.m.

Brentwood

Allanti Bicycle Co.
144 Franklin Road
Brentwood, TN 37027
(615) 373-4700
Monday–Friday, 10 a.m.–7 p.m.; Saturday, 9 a.m.–5 p.m.
www.allanti.com

Nashville

Cumberland Transit
2807 West End Avenue
Nashville, TN 37203
(615) 321-4069
Monday–Friday, 9 a.m.–7 p.m.; Saturday, 9 a.m.–6 p.m.

MOAB Bicycle Shop
8400 Highway 100 (at the northern terminus)
Nashville, TN 37221
(615) 646-2485
Monday–Friday, 10 a.m.–6 p.m.;
Saturday–Sunday, 9 a.m.–6 p.m.

Nashville Bicycle Co.
2817 West End Ave.nue #36
Nashville, TN 37203
(615) 321-5510
Monday–Saturday, 10 a.m.–6 p.m

The Parkway also has five non-vehicular campgrounds for use by bicyclers, hikers, and scouts. Consult the Appendixes (page 154) for more information.

HIKING AND HORSES

Natchez Trace National Scenic Trail

If you want to experience the Trace area the way the folks who made it famous 200 years ago did, spend some time on foot or on horseback. It's a romantic notion that you could still walk or ride the entire forested Old Trace, but you can't. Parts of the Old Trace are lost to time and nature, and some parts of it are on privately owned lands; but the paved Parkway does coincide with a small portion of the old path.

The NPS has made strides to accommodate those who'd rather make their way on foot. The Natchez Trace National Scenic Trail was established on March 28, 1983 as a unit of the National Trails System. The original plan called for 694 miles, and there are at present 63 miles of trail open for use in four areas along the Natchez Trace Parkway.

Fairly easy, with few elevation changes and no major obstacles, these trails have been built and maintained primarily by members of the Natchez Trace Trail Conference, Vicksburg Trail Dusters, Student Conservation Association, Boy Scouts of America, and other volunteers. The sections listed below have staging areas for horseback riders. The NPS has recently surveyed all the Scenic Trail miles with GPS software, and updated, precise maps should be available by the time you read this. Contact the Tupelo headquarters for more information.

Portions of the trail follow sections of the original historic Natchez Trace. Hiking and horseback riding along the trail will take you through areas of rolling hills, meadows, pine and hardwood forests, steep ravines, and some creek crossings. The trail is marked with white rectangular or oblique triangle blazes. Side, spur, and loop trails are blazed in blue. Sections of the trail follow along the Parkway road shoulder, interstates, and state roads. Please use extreme caution when traveling or crossing in these sections.

Be aware that the Parkway right-of-way line, blazed in yellow and marked by signs, is quite narrow, and the trail route often passes very close to this line, which is immediately adjacent to private property. Please respect property owners' rights along the trail route. Specific trail information may be obtained from trail brochures on each of the designed open sections. These brochures will provide information on the general area, accommodations, and directions to the trailheads.

Rules for the Natchez Trace National Scenic Trail:

▲ Heavy rains can produce muddy trail conditions, but remain on the trail and tread as lightly as possible to prevent further erosion.

▲ Overnight camping requires a special-use permit. Contact the Permit Officer at Parkway Headquarters by calling (662) 680-4014 or (800) 305-7417.

▲ Carry out all litter.

▲ No campfires are permitted.

▲ Stay on designated trails.

▲ No fireworks or firearms are permitted.

▲ Pets must be on a six-foot-or-less leash and under physical control at all times.

▲ All motorized vehicles and bicycles are prohibited.

▲ Drink water only from designated sources.

"

it's a romantic notion that you could still walk or ride the entire forested Old Trace, but you can't

"

The Natchez Trace National Scenic Trail sections open for use:

▲ Near Port Gibson, Mississippi, the **Rocky Springs section** of trail in the Port Gibson district has 10 miles open for use extending from the Regantown Road trailhead (milepost 59) south to Russell Road (milepost 50.8).

▲ The **Ridgeland district,** near Ridgeland, Mississippi, has 22 miles of trail open for use extending from the Yockanookany pull-off and picnic area (milepost 131) south to the West Florida Boundary (milepost 108).

▲ The **Tupelo district** in Tupelo, Mississippi has 7 miles of trail open for use extending from the Beech Springs parking area (milepost 266) to Chickasaw Village (milepost 261.8).

▲ At the northern end of the Parkway there are 24 miles of trail within the **Leipers Fork district,** near Franklin, Tennessee, extending from the Garrison Creek parking area (milepost 427.6) south to Tennessee Highway 50 (milepost 408).

Horseback Riding Specifics

Horseback riding is prohibited along the entire length of the Parkway except on established horse trails. The five horse trails listed below vary in length by sections from 3.5 miles to 25 miles in length and are either one-way, circle, or elongated figure-eight trails.

Horse trailers are permitted on the parkway when used noncommercially to transport horses for recreational riding, and must be properly equipped with red taillights, red stoplights, and mechanical turn signals. Clearance lights are required on trailers more than six feet high.

Trailers carrying more than one ton must be properly equipped with brakes designed to be applied by the driver of a towing motor vehicle from its cab and so connected that in case of an accidental breakaway of the towed vehicle the brakes would be applied automatically.

All trailers must be connected to the towing vehicle by means of a safety chain or equivalent device and may not exceed a total length of 55 feet in conjunction with the towing vehicle.

General information related to all trails

▲ Horse trails go through mostly wooded terrain.

▲ There are no overnight accommodations for those with horses, so the trails are for day-use only.

▲ Horses are not permitted in camping or picnicking areas.

▲ There are no horse rental facilities along the Parkway.

▲ Use caution when you must cross the Parkway.

Natchez Trace National Scenic Trail: Rocky Springs Segment

This 10-mile steep and challenging horse trail crosses creeks and ravines. The trail traverses the National Scenic Trail at milepost 59 (Reganton Road). Access to the trailhead is just off Russell Road (staging and gravel parking area), or the private Sand Creek Campground.

Natchez Trace National Scenic Trail: Ridgeland Segment

A horse trail 23 miles in length is located at Ridgeland, Mississippi. Access to this one-way trail can be gained from the Parkway at MS 43 (milepost 114.9). A graveled parking area with limited space is provided on the north access leg of MS 43. Travel north (16 miles) or south (approximately 7 miles).

Witch Dance Horse Trail in the Tombigbee National Forest

An elongated figure-eight horse trail, 9 or 15 miles in length respectively, is located almost entirely in the Tombigbee National Forest (phone (662) 285-3264), adjacent to the Natchez Trace Parkway. Access can be gained from the Parkway at the Witch Dance trailhead and picnic area (milepost 233.2), located 6 miles south of MS 32 or 4 miles north of MS 8. A paved parking and staging area is provided opposite the comfort station.

Natchez Trace National Scenic Trail: Tupelo Segment

This horse trail, 3.5 miles in length, is located northwest of Tupelo, Mississippi, within the boundaries of the Parkway. Access this looped trail from the Parkway at MS 6 (milepost 259.7 or 260.0). Travel west on MS 6 to Air Park Road, turn north (right), then east (right) on Jackson Street. A paved parking and staging area is on the left.

Natchez Trace National Scenic Trail: Leipers Fork Segment

The horse trail, approximately 25 miles in length, is located 1 mile south of TN 46 near the Leipers Fork Community, within the boundaries of the Natchez Trace Parkway. The trail parallels the Parkway from the Garrison Creek comfort station (milepost 427.6) parking and

A portion of the original Old Trace at milepost 198.6

staging area to TN 50 (milepost 408.0) parking and staging area. The only other trail access is at the TN 7, near milepost 415.6.

Milepost Self-guided Trails

The self-guided trails you encounter along the milepost stops are pleasant, often charming leg stretches, but no self-respecting hiker or even walker would suggest they are anything more than that. Most take a maximum of 15–30 minutes to experience in full-throttle stroll.

There are, however, some other hiking opportunities linked to milepost stops. From south to north (mileposts in parentheses) they are:

▲ Coles Creek (17.0) Follow the path of the Old Trace for 3.5 miles through flat lowland forest.

- ▲ Rocky Springs (55.0) At times following the Old Trace, this trail lets you walk 10 miles and reach the Owens Creek waterfall. The terrain has some roll to it, but nothing strenuous.

- ▲ Jeff Busby (193.0) A 1-mile trek to the overlook at Little Mountain has a few uphill stretches, but since the trail is short it is moderate in difficulty. One option is to walk along the road to the same vista.

- ▲ Witch Dance (233.0) has more than 10 miles of trails that can be shared with horses, which have a tendency to leave a rough surface for human feet, especially after a good rain.

- ▲ Parkway Headquarters at Tupelo (266.0) has a 4.5-mile trail that connects to the Old Town Overlook (263.9) and then goes on to the Chickasaw Village site (261.8). The terrain is flat past fields and into forests.

- ▲ Tishomingo State Park (303.0) has 13 miles of trails that explore these southern foothills of the Appalachian Mountains. This section has massive rocks that are unusual for the Trace area, as well as mature hardwoods. Hike along Bear Creek, or explore ridge tops with moderate difficulty.

- ▲ Meriwether Lewis (386.0) has more than 5 miles of trails, some of which run concurrently with the Old Trace. The terrain is made of ridges and hollows along Little Swan Creek for a moderately difficult rating.

- ▲ Devil's Backbone State Natural Area (394.0) has more than 3 miles of trails through a hardwood forest. Traversing ridges and valleys, this trail is moderately difficult and includes creeks and waterfalls.

- ▲ Garrison Creek (428.0) has 25 miles of moderately difficult trails (shared with horses) that climb ridges, overlook fields, and ford creeks.

Nearby State Park Hiking Trails

In addition to the sites above, these state parks along the Trace offer hiking trails. The first three are easy to negotiate.

- ▲ Natchez State Park has several trails that are out-and-back, old logging roads. They range in length one-way from 0.25 to 2.8 miles.

- ▲ Trace State Park has 25 miles of trails shared with ATVs, dirt bikes, mountain bikes, and horses.

- ▲ Tombigbee State Park has three nature trails that vary in length from 0.5 to 1.2 miles.

▲ David Crockett State Park has 5 miles of trails including a paved bike trail and hiking through a maple-and-oak forest with some steep climbs, making it moderately difficult.

For more detailed information about hikes in the Tennessee section of the Trace consult Johnny Molloy's *60 Hikes within 60 Miles: Nashville,* published by Menasha Ridge Press.

WATER

Many of the milepost stops have a water element. Most, however, are for visual delight rather than immersion, but there are some good creeks where you can "chill your dogs" on a hot summer day by wading or dangling your toes from a sunny rock perch.

There are at least two old-fashioned swimming holes along the Parkway. Owens Creek Falls (milepost 53.4) has two falls, the second of which is usually deep enough for a dip. The second one, Metal Ford (milepost 382.8) is a fairly broad, flat-bottom stretch of the Buffalo River.

As for canoeing, there are several possibilities. If you've got your own boat, River Bend (milepost 122.6) is a flat-water paddle option to poke about in a swampy area. It's at the northern end of the largest lake along the Parkway, the Ross Barnett Reservoir. For more information about paddling in Mississippi, contact Buffalo Peak Outfitters, 115 Highland Village, Jackson, Mississippi 39211; phone (601) 366-2557 or (800) 232-2503; fax (601) 982-1645; info@buffalopeak.net.

Tishomingo State Park (milepost 304.5) offers the Bear Creek Float Trip in warmer months. This 6.25-mile float trip down rocky-bottomed Bear Creek operates daily from mid-April until mid-October. The trips leave from the swinging bridge at 9 a.m. and 1 p.m. Visitors must register at the park office 30 minutes prior to departure. Participants return to the swinging bridge approximately two-and-a-half to three hours later. The cost is $20 per person.

Toward the northern end of the Parkway, Tennessee's Buffalo River is considered a wonderfully scenic, Class I–II stream. For Buffalo outfitters in the Linden–Hohenwald area (exit milepost 385.9 Meriwether Lewis and head west on TN 20), go to **www.thetent.com/arcadia/ tn/tnrv_buffaloriver.htm,** where "Arcadian Outdoor Guide to Canoeing, Kayaking, and Rafting Outfitters in

"
there are at least two old-fashioned swimming holes along the Parkway
"

Tennessee" can give you some leads on how to organize your trip.

At the northern terminus, Viaje (pronounced vee-ah-hey, from the Spanish "viajar" meaning to journey, travel, or tour) Outdoors rents canoes and kayaks for float trips on the Class I–II Harpeth River. They are located at the Loveless Café complex (next door to MOAB Bicycle Shop). *Viaje Outdoors, 8400 TN 100, Nashville, TN 37221; (615) 673-9239; **www.viajeoutdoors.com/home.shtml**. Wednesday–Friday, 10 a.m.–4 p.m.; Saturday–Sunday, 9 a.m.–3 p.m.*

For a host of water recreation options, including fishing, sailing, and water skiing, check out the Ross Barnett Reservoir just north of Jackson, Mississippi. For more information go to **www.rossbarnettreservoir.org,** and check out milepost 105.6 in Chapter Five "Sight-seeing by Milepost." The Tennessee River at Colbert Ferry, milepost 327.3, also has boat launches.

And we would be remiss not to mention just watching the mighty Mississippi at Natchez or Vicksburg.

ACCESSIBLE AREAS FOR THE DISABLED

The Parkway is a mixed bag when it comes to accessibility for the disabled. One advantage is that much of the Trace can be experienced, to a fair degree, from a car, but only a few of the self-guided trails are paved so they can be negotiated by those who have limited mobility or are in a wheelchair. Rather than elevation changes, the impediment here is usually rough surfaces. The good news is that usually the self-guided trails are so short it would be easy for a mobile companion to do quick reconnaissance.

Most rest rooms are accessible, as are all parking areas at the visitor center and contact stations.

(On following page)
The family cemetery at Mount Locust (milepost 15.5)

Chapter Four

A Chronology of the Natchez Trace

● ●

1540–1541   Hernando de Soto spends part of the winter in Chicka-saw villages.

1682, March 23–26   René Robert Cavelier, Sieur de LaSalle visits village of the Natchez tribe.

1699   South Carolinian begins trade with the Chickasaw.

1700   Iberville, governor of Louisiana, visits the Natchez Indian tribe.

1710   Unknown French trader sets up business at French Lick, site of Nashville.

1716, August   Fort Rosalie is built at Natchez by Jean Baptiste Le Moyne, Sieur de Bienville.

1718   St. Catherine Concession organizes, and the French begin to develop several plantations near Natchez.

1729, November 28   Natchez Indians massacre the French colony at Natchez.

1730–1731   Natchez tribe defeat and scatter. Choctaw went to help the French at Natchez. First recorded trip over any part of the Natchez Trace.

1736, May 25 Great French effort tries to destroy Chickasaw, but D'Artaguette is defeated at Ogoula Tchetota as is Bienville at Ackia.

1739, June–1740, March French lead an expedition against the Chickasaw. One hundred French Canadians with native Indian allies travel from Montreal to Tupelo.

1748–1752 Choctaw Civil War. South Carolina attempts to bring Choctaw under British control.

1763, February 10 France cedes North American possessions east of the Mississippi River, except New Orleans, including the Natchez District, to Great Britain. Spain cedes Florida to Great Britain.

1764, February 16 Natchez becomes a part of the British Colony of West Florida.

1765–1779 English-speaking people, veterans of the French and Indian War, and exiled Tories from the 13 original colonies colonize the Natchez district.

1770 John McIntosh, British agent to Chickasaw and Choctaw Indians, establishes his agency, Tockshish, or McIntoshville, 10 miles south of Pontotoc.

1775–1783 American Revolution marks the struggle by which the 13 colonies won independence from Great Britain. The fighting ended when Cornwallis surrenders at Yorktown in October.

1779, September 21 Spanish Colonial forces occupie Natchez.

1779–1782 Mount Locust plantation is built on a Spanish land grant near Natchez.

1780, April 24 Nashville is established by Richard Henderson, John Donelson, James Robertson, and other North Carolina settlers.

1781, April 22 English-speaking settlers in Natchez revolt against Spain.

1782 Americans of Cumberland settlement and Chickasaw Indians create an alliance.

1783, September 3 Treaty of Paris ends the American Revolution and recognizes the United States as a nation. The Mississippi River becomes the western boundary of the United States. East and West Florida is ceded to Spain. Spain and the United States begin a boundary quarrel.

1785 First cargo of American goods reaches Natchez via the Ohio and Mississippi rivers. The first of thousands of boatmen begin their journey over the Natchez Trace to Nashville and other areas in the Ohio Valley.

Chachare, a French officer in Spanish service, makes the trip from Natchez to Nashville on the Natchez Trace. His is the first written report of a complete journey over the Trace.

1790, May 26 Tennessee, with tentative name "Territory Southwest of the Ohio River," is organized as a Territory of the United States.

1792, March 13 Stephen Minor's trip on the Natchez Trace results in a detailed diary.

1795, October 27 By Pinchney's Treaty, Spain agrees to the 31st parallel as the southern boundary of the United States.

First cotton gin comes to Natchez.

1796, June 1 Tennessee is admitted to the Union.

1798, March 30 Spain withdraws troops, and U.S. forces occupy the Natchez District.

April 7 Mississippi Territory is organized with Natchez as capital.

1800, April 28 Congress establishes post route between Nashville and Natchez.

1801, October 24 Treaty of Chickasaw Bluffs in which the Chickasaw agree that United States can open a road, the Natchez Trace, through their lands.

December 12 Capital of Mississippi Territory moves from Natchez to Ishington, Mississippi.

December 17 Treaty of Fort Adams officially opens Old Natchez District to settlement, and the Choctaw agree that United States. may open a road, the Natchez Trace, through their lands.

1801–1802 United States troops open the Natchez Trace from Davidson–Williamson County line in Tennessee to Grindstone Ford in Mississippi.

1802, June 11 The Old Trace in Tennessee between Nashville and Duck River Ridge is abandoned as a post road.

December 27 Ferry across Tennessee River is established by George Colbert. Red Bluff Stand is established by William Smith in Mississippi. Gordon's Ferry is established on Duck River in Tennessee by John Gordon.

1803 Port Gibson, Mississippi is established.

The Regiment of Tennessee Militia marches on the Trace to and from Natchez.

1804 Mississippi Territorial boundary extends north to the Tennessee Line.

February 8 The notorious Trace outlaw, Wiley "Little" Harpe, is executed.

1805, July 23 The Chickasaw cede Tennessee lands between Duck River Ridge and Buffalo-Duck River watershed to the United States The Old Trace, from Duck River Ridge to Meriwether Lewis, becomes the boundary between the United States. and Chickasaw lands.

November 16 At the Treaty of Mt. Dexter the Choctaw cede their lands south of Old Three–Chopped Way to the United States.

1806, April 21 First Congressional appropriation is made for the improvement of the Natchez Trace.

December 2 Brashears Stand is established by Turner Brashears who lived among the Choctaw Indians in Mississippi as a trader for nearly 20 years.

1807, January 17 Aaron Burr is arrested near Natchez.

Silas Dinsmore moves the Choctaw Agency to site on the Natchez Trace.

1808 Trace between Duck River Ridge and Buffalo River is abandoned as post route.

1809, October 11 Meriwether Lewis dies and is buried at Grinders Inn along the Old Trace in Tennessee.

1810, September 22 Settlers in West Florida revolt against Spanish rule.

1812, January First Mississippi River Steamboat reaches Natchez from Pittsburgh and arrives down river at New Orleans on January 10.

May 14 West Florida is added to the Mississippi Territory.

William Doak establishes Doaks Stand in Mississippi.

1812 (approximately) At French Camp, Mississippi, Louis LeFleur establishes LeFleur's Stand.

John McLish, who is part Chickasaw, establishes McLish Stand in Tennessee.

1813, February 16 General John Coffee marches a brigade of cavalry over the Trace from Nashville to Natchez.

March 25 Andrew Jackson marches with his troops from Natchez to Nashville and is given the name "Old Hickory."

1814–1815 The Natchez Trace is a vitally important link between Ishington and New Orleans when the latter is threatened by British troops and ships.

1815 After the Battle of New Orleans, Jackson's army returns in the spring to Tennessee via the Old Natchez Trace.

1815 (approximately) Steele's Iron Works begin to produce iron at a site on the Buffalo River near the Old Trace in Tennessee.

1816, September 20   Treaty of Chickasaw Council House cedes all Chickasaw lands north of the Tennessee River to the United States.

1817   March 1   Alabama Territory is organized.

December 10   Mississippi becomes the 20th state.

1818   American Board of Commissioners for Foreign Missions establishes the Choctaw Mission. John Gordon completes his house in Tennessee.

October 19   Treaty of Old Town, also known as the Jackson Purchase, cedes Chickasaw lands in Kentucky and Tennessee to the United States.

1819, December 14   Alabama becomes the 22nd state.

1820, October 18   At the Treaty of Doaks Stand representatives of the Choctaw cede 51.5 million acres of land to the United States. The Old Trace between the Buffalo River and Buzzard Roost Stand is abandoned as a post route. Monroe Station of the Chickasaw Mission is established in Pontotoc County, Mississippi.

1820–1830   Steamboat becomes the usual method of travel from Natchez to the northeast.

1821   Bethel, a station of the Choctaw Mission, is established.

1822   The Old Trace between Brashears Stand and Red Bluff Stand is abandoned as a post road.

1830   September 27–28. At the Treaty of Dancing Rabbit Creek representatives of the Choctaw cede all lands east of the Mississippi River to the United States and agree to move to Oklahoma.

1832, October 20   At the Treaty of Pontotoc representatives of the Chickasaw cede all lands east of the Mississippi River to the United States and agree to move to Oklahoma.

1848   State of Tennessee erects a monument at the grave of Meriwether Lewis.

1861–1865   American Civil War, also known as the War Between the States and the War of Rebellion, begins when Southern states secede and Confederate commander P. G. T. Beauregard orders his men to fire on Fort Sumter, South Carolina on April 12, 1861. Four years later, on April 9, 1865, Confederate General Robert E. Lee surrenders to Union General Ulysses S. Grant at the Appomattox, Virginia courthouse.

1863   Grant's army marches over Natchez Trace, Port Gibson to Raymond.

1864, June 10   Battle of Brices Cross Roads becomes one of CSA General Nathan Bedford Forrest's most celebrated victories.

1864 *(continued)*

July 14   Battle of Tupelo.

Part of Hood's army marches over the Natchez Trace from the Tennessee–Alabama line to Nashville. After the Battles of Nashville and Franklin, the remainder of Hood's army retreats over the Old Trace to Tupelo, Mississippi.

1909–1933   Route of Natchez Trace is marked by Daughters of the American Revolution and other organizations.

1925, February 6   Meriwether Lewis National Monument is established by Presidential Proclamation.

1929, February 21   Brices Cross Roads and Tupelo Battlefields are established as National Battlefield Sites under the War Department.

1931   Commemorative monuments are erected at Brices Cross Roads and Tupelo National Battlefields.

1933, August 10   Brices Cross Roads and Tupelo National Battlefield Sites are transferred from the War Department to the National Park Service, Department of the Interior.

1934, May 21   Congress authorizes a survey of Old Natchez Trace for possible construction of a Natchez Trace Parkway.

1937, June 30   Initial Trace construction begins with award of three grading projects in Mississippi.

1938, May 18   Natchez Trace Parkway is created as a unit of the National Park Service by Act of Congress.

August 10   Ackia Battleground National Monument, Mississippi and Meriwether Lewis National Monument, Tennessee are included in Natchez Trace Parkway by Act of Congress. Tupelo National Battlefield Site is changed to a National Battlefield, and its boundaries are modified.

1996   TN 96 double-arch bridge near Franklin is completed and dedicated, opening the last incomplete section of parkway at northern terminus end near Nashville.

2005, May 18   The final segment of the Parkway around Jackson, Mississippi is scheduled to open, thereby completing the Parkway as one seamless experience from mileposts 8.1 to 444, marking 61 years of planning and construction since the Parkway's modern genesis in 1934. Plans call for an extension into Natchez and for the construction of a visitors center at the northern terminus near Nashville.

Chapter Five

Sight-seeing
by Milepost

NATCHEZ, MISSISSIPPI

As you might expect, the city of Natchez has several important sites that relate to the Natchez Trace story. Brawling boatmen, antebellum finery, tragic trade in humans, ancient burial rituals, and the might of the Mississippi River can lure you to stay here at least a day or two. The City of Natchez's Web site (See Resources, page 135) is a good place to start. Another good way to get oriented is to contact or stop by the Natchez Visitor Center, located at 640 Canal Street, Natchez, MS 39120; phone (800) 647-6724; fax (601) 442-0814; **www.mississippi riverinfo.com/natchezvisitorreception.htm**.

Natchez is proof that geography is a powerful force. The city sits comfortably on a 200-foot bluff above the Mississippi River, a natural resource that helped bring the town to life and kept it thriving. Settled in 1716 by the French who established Fort Rosalie, Natchez is the oldest "civilized" town on the river, beating New Orleans by two years. The area was inhabited, however, for centuries prior to the French by Mississippian Indians, known as Moundbuilders, and by their descendants, the Natchez.

*Before the Civil War there were 35 millionaires in the entire
United States, and Natchez had 12 of them.*

—Varina Buntin, a descendant

Whether or not that statement is precisely true, wandering
around Natchez there's plenty of evidence to support the notion.
The antebellum years in Natchez were a time of plenty: plenty
wretched for those sold at the slave market and never finer for
those who were growing and trading cotton. Try to coincide
your time in Natchez with the Spring or Fall Pilgrimage when
you can take tours of the grander homes in Natchez that now
provide an economic lifeline to the city. Tours of the homes,
which are still inhabited, are conducted by the present owners, a
charming group of people who are proud to open their
dwellings and inform you of the buildings' histories. If you like
antique furnishings, you should definitely take advantage of
these tours.

If you find yourself in Natchez at an off-Pilgrimage time,
you can still tour several historic homes, including the grand
mama of them all, Stanton Hall, maintained by the Pilgrimage
Garden Club as its headquarters and as a historic house. Built
in 1857 by Frederick Stanton, **Stanton Hall** is one of the
region's most visited National Historic Landmarks. Its scale is
pleasantly overwhelming. For example, the arched entry hall is
72 feet long, ceilings are 16.5 feet high, and the other rooms
have similar proportions. The trees that grace the grounds of
Stanton Hall's city block are century-old live oaks. Out back,
the Carriage House Restaurant and Lounge specializes in

After the Natchez attacked Fort Rosalie, the French retaliated by essentially decimating the Natchez tribe.

After France, Natchez came under the jurisdictions of
England (1763), Spain (1779), and the United States
(1795). Natchez was capital of the U.S. Mississippi Territory from 1798 to 1802. With the advent of the
steamboat to export cotton, Natchez became a great
river port and the cultural center of the planter aristoc-
racy before the Civil War. Money flowed like the water
in the river, and it built stately mansions for the planter
class. In *Life on the Mississippi,* Mark Twain remembered
the city as such:

*Natchez-on-top-of-the-Hill is attractive; has always been
attractive. Even Mrs. Trollope (1827) had to confess its
charms: "At one or two points the wearisome level line is
relieved by bluffs, as they call the short intervals of high ground.
The town of Natchez is beautifully situated on one of those*

Southern fried chicken and refreshing, smashing mint juleps.

Stanton Hall is located at High Street and Pearl Street. Open daily, 9 a.m.–5 p.m. Admission is $8. Phone (800) 647-6742 or http://natchezpilgrimage.com. Purchase tickets for the fall and spring private home viewings through Natchez Pilgrimage Tours, P. 0. Box 347, Natchez, MS 39121. Phone (601) 446-6631 or (800) 647-6742. A three-house tour, which fills a leisurely morning, costs $21. Other tour combinations are available.

If you don't have the time or the money to do a Pilgrimage tour, make **Melrose,** one of the original pilgrimage homes (now operated by the National Park Service), your one stop to understanding the scope and scale of Natchez plantation life. In addition to the big house, Melrose still has intact outbuildings, including the kitchen, laundry, slave quarters, stable, and carriage house, plus a formal garden and slavery exhibit. An important part of the Melrose's history is the story of former slaves Jane Johnson and Alice Sims, who preserved the house during a long period when it was otherwise unoccupied.

The fee for the ranger-guided tour is $6.00, unless you have a National Parks Pass (an annual fee of $50 provides admission to any National Park requiring an entrance fee and, where a per-vehicle fee is required, admits you and any accompanying passengers in your vehicle. It will also admit spouse, parents, and children at those parks where a per-visitor fee is required).

Melrose is on the Melrose Montebello Parkway. Open daily 9 a.m.–4 p.m. Phone (601) 442-7047. Admission to the house is $6; grounds are free.

high spots. The contrast that its bright green hill forms with the dismal line of black forest that stretches on every side, the abundant growth of the pawpaw, palmetto, and orange, the copious variety of sweet-scented flowers that flourish there, all make it appear like an oasis in the desert . . .

Today Natchez relies in great part on tourists, which cannot resist the remains of its Old South magnificence and romantic charm.

The Mississippi River at Natchez-under-the-Hill

✪ TRACE TOP 20

. . . the basin of the Mississippi is the Body of the Nation. All the other parts are but members, important in themselves, yet more important in their relation to this.

—Mark Twain in *Life on the Mississippi*

The Natchez tribe is the historical link to the Mound Builders of the Mississippi valley (extending from the Gulf of Mexico into Ohio), people known for their flattop ceremonial mounds. It was the river that caused these several tribes, linked by the Muskhogean language, to be called Mississippian. At the time of the first European contact with Hernando de Soto in 1540, the Natchez, who had sketchy connections to de Soto, was a tribe of approximately 5,000, living in what is now known as the greater city of Natchez. They were in present-day southwest Mississippi for about 1,000 years, from about CE 700 to 1730. They looked to the ceremonial center at Grand Village, now a National Historic Landmark, for their religious, ceremonial, and political needs. The Natchez also built Emerald Mound, but abandoned it in favor of Grand Village.

A settled people who farmed, hunted, and fished, according to the NPS, the Natchez were "well-formed, handsome people

"Father of Waters," as some Native Americans called the Mississippi, is one of the longest rivers in the world. Its headwaters begin at Lake Itasca, Minnesota, where the river is between 20 and 30 feet wide and about 3 feet deep. Heading south, the Mississippi merges and meanders for a length of more than 2,300 miles until it empties into the Gulf of Mexico at New Orleans and reaches a depth of 200 feet.

Measurements of the river's length vary because the river is in a constant state of change. The Mississippi is, however, the third-largest watershed in the world. The combined length of the Mississippi and the Missouri, which flow together in St. Louis, make the Mississippi the fourth-longest river in the world after the Nile, Amazon, and Yangtze.

Viewing the river at Natchez from near the bridge at the Natchez Visitor Center, you have a broad view of the delta's dirt drifting toward the Gulf. It is worth the drive across the bridge to the Comfort Suites Riverfront hotel in Vidalia, Louisiana, where you can enjoy a meal in the open air, have a view of the Natchez bluff, and watch the weight of the world float by.

The Mississippi carries close to half a million pounds of sediment with it every day of the year. Some geologists think that the waters of the Gulf of Mexico once reached as far north as Cairo, Illinois, meaning that over eons, the silting process may have created the land mass that is the south-central United States.

> "
> the combined length of the Mississippi and the Missouri, which flow together in St. Louis, make the Mississippi the fourth-longest river in the world after the Nile, Amazon, and Yangtze
> "

with dark copper skin, coarse black hair, and black eyes." They practiced head flattening (carrying infants on a rigid board to shape their skulls while still malleable), blackened their teeth with tobacco and wood ashes, and favored tattoos. They are noted for their excellent hand-molded pottery, and fire-crafted canoes that sometimes measured 3 feet by 40 feet.

Encouraged by the English, who were enemies of France, the Natchez massacred the French people at Fort Rosalie at dawn on November. 28, 1729. French troops retaliated, and with the aid of Creek warriors, obliterated the tribe. A few Natchez escaped and were assimilated into the Chickasaw and Cherokee tribes. Some were sold into slavery in British West India. The very few Natchez descendents live now in Oklahoma and in the Appalachian Mountains.

The Mississippi River made the Natchez Trace into the important highway home for the "Kaintuck" boatmen who had floated their goods down to Natchez. Unofficially the Trace begins at Natchez-Under-the-Hill on the banks of the Mississippi. This is where the nineteenth-century flatboats and steamboats landed. Once a notorious area where suddenly wealthy flatboat captains flaunted their riches on women and liquor, the area today features trendy gift shops and a few open-air restaurants. It's a good place to begin your journey. Natchez-Under-the-Hill is now a historic strip of buildings tucked under the bluff, easily accessible by car.

The Mississippi River is hypnotizing. Watch it for ten minutes and you can sense its majesty and muscle. Essentially untamable, it is still prone to flooding. As Tennessee historian Ann Toplovich wrote, "One of the world's natural wonders, the Mississippi River system looms large in the history and culture . . . and residents living along its banks continue to search for ways to live in harmony with its strength."

Grand Village of the Natchez Indians

The Natchez mounds that survive today at Grand Village are, in several ways, like the cathedrals of Europe. Their construction consecrated holy ground in stages, probably beginning in the 1200s CE, around the same time that construction began on Chartres Cathedral in France. Grand Village was the center of life for the

✪ TRACE TOP 20

———

ARCHEOLOGY AND
NATIVE AMERICANS

*Slaves! Slaves! Slaves! Forks of the Road, Natchez . . . just
arrived . . . a choice selection of mechanics, field hands, cooks,
washers and ironers, and general house servants.*

—November 27, 1858
Natchez Daily Courier advertisement

Traffic headed north on the Trace, mainly the "Kaintuck" boatmen, began to decline with the advent of the steamboat era in
the early 1820s. But around the same time a new kind of traffic,
enslaved humans, began tramping the Trace heading south from
Nashville to Natchez. Although in 1808 federal law prohibited
importing Africans for the slave market, there was a steady supply of slaves in the Chesapeake Bay–area on aging tobacco plantations. As demand for cotton by European textile mills began
to eclipse tobacco, the market for slaves began to weaken in
Maryland and Virginia and grow stronger in the Deep South.
For example, in 1825–1830 the average price in Virginia for a
young male adult was $400. In Natchez, it was $560.

Natchez ranked second to New Orleans nationally as a slave
market. The undisputed prominent place to buy slaves in

Natchez from at least 1682 until 1729, when the tribe
provoked war with the French and was subsequently
destroyed as a people.

At Grand Village you can observe a broad field and
walk its circuit, studying at your leisure the reconstructed house and granary; a mound abandoned *probably due to erosion from St. Catherine's Creek; the
prehistoric and historic ceremonial plazas; the Great
Sun's Mound; and the Temple Mound. Much more than
just hills of dirt, these mounds hold the memories of
many dramatic and sometimes deadly events.

While the great majority of the tribe lived on nearby
farms, the chief, known as the Great Sun, lived at Grand
Village on the prominent, centrally located mound. Here
an inner sanctum housed the perpetual sacred fire, sym-
bolic of the sun from which the royal family had
descended. The male or female Great Sun was worshipped
as a living embodiment of the divine sun, and had the
power of life and death over the other people. The Great
Sun came to assume the position through matrilineal
descent. Upon his or her death the dead Sun's family, servants, and friends and warriors who so desired were
sedated and then strangled during the burial ceremony.

Beyond the drama of death rituals, you can sit on the
Great Sun's mound and consider the earth in much the

"

*the male or female
Great Sun was worshipped
as a living embodiment
of the divine sun, and had
the power of life and death
over the other people*

"

Natchez was at a crossroads just outside the city limits, called Forks of the Road. Remembered now with a historical marker, it was then within sight of mansions known today as Devereux, Linden, and Monmouth, grand homes that are often on the Natchez Pilgrimage tours.

Forks of the Road was a casual market that eschewed the public agitation of an auction, favoring quiet deals among buyers and sellers. In the 1830s and early 1840s, Franklin and Armfield, the most active slave traders in the United States, moved slaves overland on the Natchez Trace to Forks of the Road. In the 1830s they were sending more than 1,000 slaves annually from Alexandria, Virginia to their Natchez and New Orleans markets. At its peak, Forks of the Road had as many as 500 people for sale at one time. All this came to a halt in 1863 when Union troops occupied Natchez that summer.

The Forks of the Road was located at the intersection of Liberty and Washington Roads. Now Washington Road is called Devereux Drive, and it changes to St. Catherine Street at the Liberty Road intersection.

same way that the Great Sun did—through the natural elements. You can also empathize with the responsibilities of leadership, and of the difficulties to decide to launch an attack on the ever-encroaching French, a decision that ultimately resulted in the loss of virtually everything and everyone, leaving only these mute mounds as witness.

Grand Village of the Natchez Indians, 400 Jefferson Davis Boulevard, Natchez, MS 39120. Phone (660) 446-6502. Museum, gift shop, nature trails, and mound site. Monday–Saturday, 9 a.m.–5 p.m.; Sunday, 1:30–5 p.m. Free admission. In Natchez, turn east off US 61/Seagent S. Prentiss Drive onto Jefferson Davis Boulevard, just south of the Natchez Regional Medical Center. Proceed on Jefferson Davis Boulevard a half mile. The entrance gate is on the right.

MISSISSIPPI MILEPOSTS

NATCHEZ, MISSISSIPPI TO JACKSON, MISSISSIPPI

Plans call for the extension of the Parkway into Natchez proper, probably designating river landing Natchez-under-the-Hill as the official starting point. For now the **Natchez Visitor Reception Center,** 640 South Canal Street, serves as the de facto welcoming station.

To find the visitor center, head toward the bridge (US 61-65-84) that spans the Mississippi into Vidalia, Louisiana. It's the modern building on the right, but access is from Canal Street (US 84) that runs parallel to the river on the bluff. Open Monday–Saturday, 8:30 a.m.–6 p.m.; Sunday, 9 a.m.–4 p.m. Phone (800) 647-6724; **www.cityofnatchez.com.** *Free exhibits, gift shop, bookstore. Audio-video orientation presentation admission, $2.*

To get on the Natchez Trace Parkway, head north on US 61 until you see signs for the Natchez Trace Parkway. The signs will direct you to turn right onto Liberty Road which will connect you to the southern end of the Parkway. As you travel north on the Parkway, you will come to the Elizabeth Female Academy on your left.

4.8 Elizabeth Female Academy

This distinguished school, operating from 1818 to 1845, was the first institution of higher learning for women chartered by the state of Mississippi. As such it represented progressive thinking as well as the needs of an emerging upper class that desired cultural refinements for their daughters. Varina Howell, who married the future Confederacy's president Jefferson Davis, was a graduate.

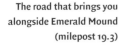

The road that brings you alongside Emerald Mound (milepost 19.3)

After visiting the Academy continue north for a couple of miles to US 61. If you get off the Parkway here

and travel south about 3 miles, you will pass through Washington, Mississippi's first state capitol city where you can visit **Historic Jefferson College.** Jefferson College opened on January 7, 1811. Named after President Thomas Jefferson, it was the first educational institution of higher learning in Mississippi, and it became the focal point of a thriving antebellum intellectual community. Noted naturalist John James Audubon taught at both Elizabeth Female Academy and Historic Jefferson College in 1822 to 1823 while he recorded the birds of the Lower Mississippi region.

Historic Jefferson College is administered by the Mississippi Department of Archives and History. Buildings, Monday–Saturday, 9 a.m.–5 p.m.; Sunday, 1–5 p.m. Grounds, sunup–sundown. Phone (601) 442-2901. Admission is free. Almost immediately after Historic Jefferson College you will see the familiar brown signs directing you onto the Natchez Trace Parkway.

8.7 Old Trace Exhibit Shelter

Heading north, this is your first glimpse at the Old Trace, so stop and take a look. Depending on the time of year and the thickness of the foliage, you can walk about 100 yards before the brush becomes forbidding in late spring. This section gives you a sense of the sunken quality the old road sometimes has, having been worn down by animals over thousands of years. It also hints at the uneven surface that would have been daunting and disabling to humans when extended over nearly 500 miles.

10.3 Emerald Mound

If you are impressed by scale, you will love Emerald Mound. Now named for the Emerald Plantation whose acreage once encompassed it, the mound staggers the imagination with its scale when you contemplate its construction. The nation's second-largest Mississippian structure, Emerald covers nearly eight acres and is superceded only by Monk's Mound at the famous Cahokia, Illinois site. Emerald Mound measures 770 feet by 435 feet at its base (roughly 2.5 by 1.5 football fields), and is approximately 35 feet high.

Ancestors of the Natchez built and used this ceremonial mound from about CE 1250 to 1600. For reasons unknown, after that time the Mississippian Indians who built it shifted their ceremonial center to Grand Village. A subject of archeological investigations beginning in 1838, the mound was built by depositing earth along

In 1541 the Spanish explorer Hernando de Soto and his men were the first Europeans to intrude upon the Native Americans living along the Natchez Trace. Some 140 years later French explorer Robert Cavelier, Sieur de la Salle, visited a Natchez tribal village, perhaps at Emerald Mound, during his adventures sailing down the Mississippi River to its mouth at the Gulf of Mexico. Subsequently, he not-so-modestly claimed the entire Mississippi River valley for France. In 1699, France's claim was reasserted by Pierre le Moyne, Sieur d'Iberville, who established a trading relationship with the Natchez. The French strengthened their hold by building Fort Rosalie in present-day Natchez on the grounds of what later became Rosalie Mansion.

The Natchez rebelled at the increasing French presence by attacking the fort, killing 250 men, and taking 300 women and children prisoners. Within weeks the French retaliated and destroyed the Natchez tribe, the first group to suffer enormous losses at the hands of the Europeans. Eager to assert themselves further into the region, the French led an attack on the Chickasaw six years later, in 1736, near the village of Ackia. They were joined by the Choctaw, traditional enemies of the Chickasaw.

the sides of a natural hill. When you consider that in southern Mississippi you are not exactly in "hill country," the scope of labor and intent to build Emerald Mound begins to take shape. It took a powerfully organized society to build a structure such as this.

Take the trail to the top, an easy ascent, and you will find two more mounds at either end, both impressive as stand-alone structures. The larger one measures 190 by 160 feet at the base and 30 feet in height. Early drawings suggest there may also have been four or six smaller mounds along the edges. When you approach and ascend Emerald Mound you are on consecrated ground, for here elaborate civic processions, ceremonial dances, and intricate and solemn religious rituals were conducted.

Reached by exiting the Parkway at milepost 10.3 at the Route 553 intersection. Follow the signs for about a mile down an increasingly rural road.

NATURAL WONDERS

12.1 Turpin Creek

There is a picnic area alongside the road.

NATURAL WONDERS

12.4 Loess Bluff

What appears to be a fairly nondescript exposed hillside is actually a glimpse of a geologic process that began dur-

However, the Chickasaw, with some support from the British in the form of supplies, soundly defeated the invaders, and France's importance in the region began to wane.

According to the first Treaty of Paris, in 1763 England claimed France's possessions east of the Mississippi. The English rebuilt Fort Rosalie, renaming it Fort Panmure. The English held the region as British West Florida until Spain reappeared on the Gulf Coast and occupied Natchez until the late 1790s. The Second Treaty of Paris, signed in 1783 by England and the now-recognized United States, acknowledged the United States' claim to West Florida south to the 31st parallel. Spain objected, and insisted that the United States' claim stopped at the 32° 28' parallel. The dispute continued until 1795, when Spain finally accepted the more southern boundary. With Spain's eventual withdrawal from the area in 1798 when the Mississippi Territory was organized, the last European claim to the Natchez Trace region ended. The first European nation to arrive was the last to leave. Yet sunder the fledging United States' control, the impact of the various European cultures lingered for many years.

ing the Pleistocene epoch 1 million years ago. Deposits of silt (loess, pronounced like the woman's name, Lois) were blown here from the north during the Ice Age. Thick loess deposits such as this are generally found in areas where there were glaciers. As glaciers melted in the summer months, finely ground water-borne sediment formed at the edges of the glaciers. In winter, when the water stopped flowing, the winter winds carried this fine sediment in huge dust storms. As the wind died down, the silt fell to the earth, creating deposits such as the one you see here. Loess deposits are frequently most extensive and thickest downwind from large river valleys, of which the Mississippi valley certainly is one.

15.5 Mount Locust

Mount Locust is one of a kind. Of the 50 or so primitive hostelries established before 1820 along the Trace, only Mount Locust remains. It is one of the oldest buildings in Mississippi, dating to 1780. In 1956 it was restored to its form as a frontier home of the 1820s, which was the peak era of the Trace's foot and horse travel.

The core of the house was built by Swiss-born John Blommart, who had to meet the conditions of his land grant to "erect one good Dwelling House to contain at

✪ TRACE TOP 20

KAINTUCK BOATMEN
AND THE POSTAL ROAD

least twenty feet in length, sixteen feet in Breadth." After Blommart was imprisoned and then exiled for his alliance with the British against the Spanish, Blommart's business associate, William Ferguson, acquired the property and eventually increased his holdings to 1,215 acres.

While farming was Ferguson's major interest, with others he attempted to create a thriving village called Union, which was to occupy the land in front of Mount Locust. The main street of Union is still visible running parallel near the Trace. The town, which had about half a dozen buildings, began to decline after it was not chosen as the county seat and after Ferguson's death in 1801.

Ferguson's widow, Pauline, married James Chamberlain. The inn business prospered as the Trace traffic grew, for Mount Locust was a one-day walk from Natchez. Andrew Jackson reportedly stayed here twice. Among many outbuildings, a four-room, two-story annex called Sleepy Hollow was built behind the house to hold wall-to-wall corn shuck mattresses. After her husband abandoned her in 1810, Pauline carried on nobly and industriously. When she died in 1849, Mount Locust was appraised at around $50,000.

The old framework of the house is sassafras, and was found to be in almost perfect condition where the other woods had succumbed to the years of southern Mississippi's moist heat. The interior trim and walls are poplar; the exterior siding, cypress. The whitewashed front and indigo-dyed blue shutters are authentic to the period.

Ask to speak with Ranger Eric Chamberlain, who may be staffing the interpretation at the house. A direct descendant of Pauline and James Chamberlain, he was born there in 1940 and has great knowledge of Mount Locust and its varied history. Interpretive programs are given February through November.

> "
> *Andrew Jackson reportedly stayed here twice*
> "

NATURAL WONDERS

17.5 Coles Creek

This stop features a picnic area and rest rooms.

NATURAL WONDERS

18.4 Bullen Creek

The parkway offers numerous opportunities for a simple and relatively short leg stretch. At Bullen Creek a flat, self-guided trail leads through a mixed hardwood-pine forest. The walk takes 15 minutes if you just stroll.

21.0 Springfield Plantation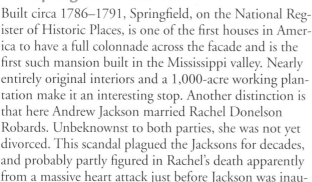

Built circa 1786–1791, Springfield, on the National Register of Historic Places, is one of the first houses in America to have a full colonnade across the facade and is the first such mansion built in the Mississippi valley. Nearly entirely original interiors and a 1,000-acre working plantation make it an interesting stop. Another distinction is that here Andrew Jackson married Rachel Donelson Robards. Unbeknownst to both parties, she was not yet divorced. This scandal plagued the Jacksons for decades, and probably partly figured in Rachel's death apparently from a massive heart attack just before Jackson was inaugurated as the seventh U.S. president.

Take MS 553 to Fayette; Springfield Plantation is one mile from the Parkway. 8733 River Road 553, South Fayette, MS 39069. Open year-round except Christmas Day; Monday–Saturday, 9:30 a.m.–sunset; Sunday, 10:30 a.m.–sunset. Hours may vary November 15–March 1; call owner and proprietor Arthur E. LaSalle in advance at (601) 786-3802.

30.0 Windsor Ruins

✪ TRACE TOP 20

KAINTUCK BOATMEN
AND THE POSTAL ROAD

One of the most visually stunning detours off the parkway takes you to the ghostly form of an antebellum mansion. Winsdor was built by Smith Coffee Daniell II—begun in 1859 and finished in 1861—just before the Civil War began. Tragically, Mr. Daniell, who was only 34, died just a few weeks after its completion. The total cost of the mansion was $175,000, or more than $3 million by today's costs.

At its peak, the entire Windsor plantation sprawled 2,600 acres. The four-story home had 25 rooms with 25 fireplaces, and attic tanks supplied water to the interior baths. The basement floor had a school room, dairy, and supply rooms. The roof observatory was used to signal Confederate troops about Union advances. Twenty-nine 45-foot-tall columns were joined across the front with an ornamental iron balustrade. Windsor was used as a Union hospital during the Civil War and survived the conflict intact.

In an ironic turn of events, however, on February 17, 1890 a fire broke out after a party guest accidentally dropped a cigarette on the third floor in some repair debris. Windsor burned to the ground, leaving only a few pieces of china, 23 columns, and the balustrade. Windsor was immortalized in several films, including *Raintree County* with Elizabeth Taylor and Montgomery Clift. Visiting Windsor Ruins today, as it is known, is an eerie and beautiful experience. The scale of the columns points clearly to a former grandeur that the powers of fire, earth, and time have since reclaimed as their own.

Heading north on the Parkway, take MS 552 at milepost 30. Follow the signs. If you follow MS 552 on into Port Gibson, the side trip will take about 45 minutes including about 15 minutes at Windsor. 15095 Rodney Road; phone (601) 437-4351. Open daily from dawn to dusk. Admission is free.

Note: From Port Gibson you can get back on the Parkway or head north on US 61 to Vicksburg. To

Eerie, stately columns stand at Windsor Ruins (milepost 30.0)

return to the Parkway go north (left) on US 61. At the intersection of MS 18 go right. In 1 mile MS 18 intersects with the Parkway. Head north toward Jackson.

38.0 Vicksburg National Military Park

CIVIL WAR
AND OTHER
MILITARY HISTORY

The Vicksburg campaign was waged from March 29 to July 4, 1863. It included battles in west-central Mississippi at Port Gibson, Raymond, Jackson, Champion Hill, and Big Black River, and 47 days of Union siege operations against Confederate forces defending the city of Vicksburg. Located high on the bluffs, Vicksburg was a fortress guarding the Mississippi River. It was known as "The Gibraltar of the Confederacy." Its surrender on July 4, 1863, coupled with the fall of Port Hudson, Louisiana, divided the South and gave the North undisputed control of the Mississippi River.

Today, the battlefield at Vicksburg is in an excellent state of preservation. It includes 1,325 historic monuments and markers, 20 miles of reconstructed trenches and earthworks, a 16-mile tour road, an antebellum home, 144 emplaced cannon, restored Union gunboat *USS Cairo*, and the Vicksburg National Cemetery.

Vicksburg National Military Park, 3201 Clay Street, Vicksburg, MS 39183. Open daily except Christmas Day. Visitor center: 8 a.m.–5 p.m.; (601) 636-0583. Cairo Museum: November–March, 8:30 a.m.–5 p.m; April–October, 9:30 a.m–6 p.m.; (601) 636-2199; Vickinterpretation@nps.gov.

From Port Gibson, take MS 61 north. Look for the signs to Vicksburg. The Park is on the right-hand side of the road heading toward the river (west). The Mississippi Welcome Center is just across the street.

> **"**
>
> *the fortress at Vicksburg was known as 'The Gibraltar of the Confederacy'*
>
> **"**

41.0 Windsor Ruins

(See description at milepost 30). *Heading south, take MS 552 out of Port Gibson.*

✪ TRACE TOP 20
———
KAINTUCK BOATMEN
AND THE POSTAL ROAD
———
THE LIVING TRACE

41.5 Sunken Trace

This is the compelling section of the Trace featured on the front of the National Park Service map guide. This short stretch is deeply evocative and will open your imagination. Animals first wore down this path, then people.

✪ TRACE TOP 20
———
THE OLD TRACE

**Sunken Trace
(milepost 41.5)**

In fading sunlight, within these high earthen walls, it is simple to picture how easily outlaws ambushed folks moving along the Trace. On this section of the Trace you are looking at the effects of time, hooves, and feet. The trail is very short, and the Park Service recommends five minutes here, but if you linger a little longer you may sense the spirit of those who trod here before you.

KAINTUCK BOATMEN
AND THE POSTAL ROAD

———

ARCHEOLOGY AND
NATIVE AMERICANS

45.7 Grindstone Ford and Mangum Mound

Northbound travelers believed they were entering wild country when they crossed Grindstone Ford on Bayou Pierre, about 45 miles, or two-days' walk from Natchez. In fact, they were leaving the Natchez district and entering the Choctaw nation. Grindstone Ford was named for a water-driven mill nearby. This was a substantial water-crossing landmark, as Bayou Pierre is a stream that can be floated for more than 100 miles before it eventually feeds into the Mississippi River.

Mangum Mound, a subtle rise, is a remnant from the Plaquemine Indian culture, which flourished about CE 1,000 and was a forerunner of the Natchez tribe. Plaquemine Indians often built mounds on top of the ruins of a house or temple, constructing similar buildings on top of the mound. In earlier times, buildings were usually circular, but later they were likely to be rectangular. They were constructed of wattle and daub (interwoven rods and laths or twigs plastered with mud or clay), and sometimes had wall posts sunk into foot-deep wall trenches.

At times, these Indians dug shallow, oval or rectangular, graves in the mounds. They may have been for primary burials of individuals, but more frequently they were for the reburial of remains originally interred elsewhere. Excavations at Mangum Mound indicate that, similar to their Natchez descendants, the Plaquemine sacrificed infants in their death-ritual ceremonies.

52.4 Owens Creek Waterfall

NATURAL WONDERS

A water table drop has changed the flow here to just a trickle unless it has recently rained heavily, but you can still enjoy a picnic here and take the 2.5-mile hiking trail to Rocky Springs (see below).

54.8 Rocky Springs

THE OLD TRACE

———

THE LIVING TRACE

———

NPS INFORMATION

Two hundred years ago, Rocky Springs was a thriving little town whose settlement began in the 1790s and grew to several thousand at its peak in the 1850s. This is somewhat hard to imagine as you walk a short section of the Old Trace where, save for an 1837 church still in use, the chief activity is the flourishing of the green undergrowth. The homes, school, post office, and Masonic lodge that once were here are all gone. Occupation by General Grant's 40,000 Union troops in 1863; yellow fever in 1878; boll weevils in the early 1900s; and the death of the spring itself sealed Rocky Springs' fate as a ghost town. A short, easy trail from the upper parking area leads to the old town site where another short, easy loop trail carries you past two old safes, scant remnants of the life that was here until little more than a century ago. This stop features camping, picnicking, a Ranger Station, rest rooms, and a phone. (See Chapter Two, "The Nuts

Like the Natchez, the Choctaw are linked to the Mississippian mound building culture, but the link is not as obvious, nor as certain. If the Choctaw did build mounds they had long ceased to build them by the time of pioneer settlement. Still, the central legend of the Choctaw is that they originated from "Nanih Waya," a sacred hill near what is now known as Noxapter, Mississippi. "Nanih Waiya" means "Productive Mound" and is often referred to as "The Mother Mound." Women in Choctaw culture have always been honored as the head of every household.

The Choctaw were considered the best farmers of the Southeast, growing enough food to be able to barter with it. They shared many cultural practices with their neighbors, the Natchez, but their burial rituals did not require the deaths of surviving family and friends.

Death was a much more frequent companion than it is today. The Choctaw had several wars with the Chickasaw, their neighboring tribe to the north, but they also had several effective peace treaties. Some scholars think the two tribes may have been one long ago; early writers mention a "hereditary" enmity between the two. It is also possible that the rivalry between the Choctaw and the Chickasaw was aggravated by the onslaught of Europeans, who sought to "divide and conquer."

and Bolts of Traveling the Trace" (p. 29), for more information on this campground.)

and Bolts of Traveling the Trace" (p. 29), for more information on this campground.)

ARCHEOLOGY AND
NATIVE AMERICANS

61.0 Lower Choctaw Boundary

The Treaty of Doak's Stand was a crucial agreement between the U.S. government and the Native Americans living in Mississippi and Alabama. It shifted the southern Choctaw boundary from milepost 61 north to milepost 128.4. This spot on the Trace marks the lower boundary of that treaty that opened new lands for white settlement and allowed Mississippi to shift its capitol from Natchez to more-centrally-located Jackson. This treaty also set the stage for the Choctaw and Chickasaw nations to give up their homelands under threat of annihilation and move west of the Mississippi River. At Doak's Stand Andrew Jackson reportedly lost his temper at the Choctaw negotiator Pushmataha. Failing a Choctaw capitulation, Jackson promised forcible removal at best and extinction of the tribe at worst.

The relationship between the Choctaw and the white settlers is complex. The Choctaw chief Pushmataha, affirming his allegiance to the United States, led several hundred warriors with Andrew Jackson at the Battles of New Orleans and Horseshoe Bend. But the Choctaws were the first of the five great southern-U.S. tribes to be moved to Oklahoma by the Treaty of Dancing Rabbit Creek in 1830. More than 20,000 Choctaws were forced to make this long, arduous journey. Many did not survive, which is why their route is often referred to as The Trail of Tears. Although historically associated with the Cherokee, The Trail of Tears has come to represent the removal of all southeastern tribes.

Choctaw "code talkers," as they are called, were invaluable in World War I when they relied upon their linguistic heritage to create unbreakable codes. Today Choctaw live in their ancestral homelands in Mississippi as well as in Oklahoma, where the so-called Western Band long ago reestablished a thriving culture. Although not many of the surviving members of the other four great southeastern tribes—Cherokee, Chickasaw, Creek, and Seminole—now speak their native language, many Choctaw still speak their historic language today.

73.5 Deans Stand

Many farmers ran stands that were rough, rustic inns offering travelers a simple meal and a floor or a patch of dirt on which to sleep. If farmers were lucky enough to be located along the Trace, this basic service was a natural addition to their income. "Location, location, location" definitely applied. William and Margaret Dean settled here in 1823 after the Treaty of Doak's Stand negotiated settlement rights for white pioneers on Choctaw lands. This stop features a picnic area.

KAINTUCK BOATMEN
AND THE POSTAL ROAD

THE OLD TRACE

78.3 Battle of Raymond

Union General Sherman's overall plan for the western theater of the war (including parts of Tennessee and Mississippi) was to split the Confederacy in half from the Mississippi River eastward toward Savannah. This became known as "Sherman's March to the Sea." In order to protect Sherman's sole supply line from Nashville to Chattanooga, Union General Samuel Sturgis was sent to

CIVIL WAR
AND OTHER
MILITARY HISTORY

secure northwestern Mississippi, where the infamous Confederate General Nathan Forrest wreaked havoc with his raids. The Battle of Raymond, part of the Vicksburg campaign, was fought nearby. At this site on Tuesday, May 12, 1863, Confederate brigade forces, commanded by Brigadier General John Gregg, attacked the Union division, part of General Grant's forces led by Major General John A. Logan of McPherson's corps. The Confederates were driven back toward Jackson, Mississippi after several hours of fighting. About 1,000 men were killed or wounded, in a loss borne equally by the Union and the Confederacy.

JACKSON, MISSISSIPPI

> *. . . beautiful and healthful surroundings, good water, abundant timber, navigable waters, and nearness to the Natchez Trace.*
>
> —From the report to the Mississippi General Assembly recommending Jackson as the capitol city

"

Jackson was burned three times during the Civil War by General William Tecumseh Sherman's Union troops

"

The city of Jackson began as a trading post known as LeFleur's Bluff, named for French-Canadian trader Louis LeFleur. Situated on a "high handsome bluff" of the Pearl River, Jackson—named for Andrew Jackson—was founded in 1821 when the Mississippi State Legislature named it the new, more-centrally-located capitol city. The location was selected, according to a report to the General Assembly, because it had "beautiful and healthful surroundings, good water, abundant timber, navigable waters, and nearness to the Natchez Trace." Thus, the affairs of state moved from Natchez to Jackson.

Jackson was burned three times during the Civil War by General William Tecumseh Sherman's Union troops. City Hall, built in 1846, was spared the torch probably because it was serving as a hospital. This building is still the seat of Jackson's city government.

The metropolitan Jackson area has a population of more than 425,000, supporting various museums, several sites that pertain to the Civil War era and to the 1960s struggle for civil rights, as well as natural history, fine arts, and antebellum sites and institutions.

*For detailed information on lodging and attractions, contact the Jackson Convention and Visitors Bureau, P.O. Box 1450, Jackson, MS 39215; phone (800) 354-7695 or (601) 960-1891; **www.visitjackson.com**.*

93.0 Cowles Mead Cemetery

THE LIVING TRACE

Cowles (pronounced "coals") Mead was an example of those who came to what was then called "The Southwest" to follow opportunities as they presented themselves. At first a tavern owner on the Trace near Natchez, he held several political offices. As acting governor in 1806 he ordered the arrest of former vice president Aaron Burr for treason, but Burr was acquitted. As Jackson grew, Meade moved to the area and built a home, "Greenwood," at this site. After his death it burned during the Civil War, and now only a family cemetery remains.

95.0 Osburn Stand

KAINTUCK BOATMEN
AND THE POSTAL ROAD

Beginning in 1805, the Choctaw permitted inns, or "stands," to be constructed along the Trace. By 1811, Noble Osburn operated a stand here to provide basic food and shelter for Trace travelers. He had a reputation for treating U.S. citizens and native people equally.

100.0 Choctaw Agency

ARCHEOLOGY AND
NATIVE AMERICANS

From 1807 until 1820 Silas Dinsmore lived here while holding the difficult job of Choctaw agent. His responsibilities included representing the interests of the Choctaw while implementing U.S. policies. He checked passports, collected debts, and insured that the Choctaw were paid for lands ceded to the United States. He also taught farming methods. As Choctaw lands continually shrank in the face of pioneer settlement demands, the Choctaw Agency had to move four times to remain within tribal boundaries.

102.4 Mississippi Crafts Center

THE LIVING TRACE

The Craftsmen's Guild of Mississippi was founded in 1973 as a nonprofit organization of craftsmen and others interested in preserving and promoting the folk, traditional, and contemporary crafts of Mississippi. It has been located on the Natchez Trace Parkway since 1975. The center, housed in a dogtrot cabin (a style of Southern domestic architecture having two primary living spaces connected by a covered porch) features a Guild sales shop and offers a nationally recognized program of crafts demonstrations, classes, and festivals.

Works available for purchase range from centuries-old Native American cane basket designs by members of the Choctaw tribe, to pottery, weaving, quilting, and jewelry in traditional and contemporary styles. There is no admission charge, and this is an opportunity for Parkway travelers to view high-quality, handmade Mississippi wood, glass, metal, textile, and ceramic items. Facilities include picnic tables, rest rooms, bus parking, and wheelchair access.

Open year-round, seven days a week, 9 a.m.–5 p.m. Take the Natchez Trace Exit (105-A) from I-55 North, 1 mile north of Jackson, Mississippi.

JACKSON, MISSISSIPPI TO TUPELO, MISSISSIPPI

KAINTUCK BOATMEN
AND THE POSTAL ROAD
————
THE OLD TRACE

104.5 Brashear's Stand and Old Trace

The first stand allowed by the Choctaw nation was called Turner Brashear's Stand. This inn was advertised as "a house of entertainment in the wilderness" to travelers when it opened in 1806. In 1850 it was known as King's Inn, named for an associate of the infamous Murrell gang. According to legend, King robbed his wealthy guests and tossed their remains into the wilderness. Andrew Jackson visited the inn on his return from the Battle of New Orleans, and Confederate General Stephen D. Lee used it as his headquarters during the Civil War. In 1852 King's Inn became Hawthorne Vale. It was destroyed by fire in 1896 and is now only a memory. A short section of the original Trace is nearby.

NATURAL WONDERS

105.6 Ross Barnett Reservoir Overlook

The 33,000-acre Ross Barnett Reservoir on the Pearl River parallels the Parkway for 8 miles. The reservoir was created by impounding the Pearl River between Madison and Rankin Counties. Bound by the Natchez Trace on the north, it has 105 miles of shoreline.

The reservoir is named for the 52nd governor of the State of Mississippi, Ross Barnett, who was born in Leake County, Mississippi on January 22, 1898. A Democrat, Barnett served as governor of Mississippi from 1960–1966, and died November 6, 1987.

The Pearl River Valley Water Supply District, which administers the reservoir, provides recreational opportunities in the area, including 48 parks, and outdoor facilities, including 5 campgrounds, 16 parks, 22 boat launches, 3 wheelchair-accessible trails, and 2 multipurpose trails. Each campground has a live-in, on-site reservoir patrol manager. In conjunction with private and public sectors, the District has also developed five marinas, four baseball and soccer complexes, two golf courses, and a water park.

"

according to legend, King robbed his wealthy guests and tossed their remains into the wilderness

"

The view at Ross Barnett
Reservoir Overlook
(milepost 105.6)

The reservoir offers numerous places to launch a boat and paddle. The reservoir map lists all boat ramps, depth contours, structures, fishing information, and GPS points. It covers the reservoir and Pearl River from the spillway north to Tuscolameta Creek, which is just upriver from the MS 25 bridge over the Pearl River.

Contact Buffalo Peak Outfitters, phone (601) 366-2557, for a Ross Barnett Reservoir map, or download one and get more information at **www.rossbarnettreservoir.org***. For camping information or reservations call (877) 388-CAMP (2267).*

106.9 Boyd Site

Most known burial mounds in Mississippi date to the Middle Woodland times (circa BCE 100–CE 400). The six small burial mounds at the Boyd site, however, were built much later, during the Late Woodland and Early Mississippian periods, circa CE 800–1100 (900 to 1,200 years ago). One of these, Mound 2, is accessible to visitors.

Several of the mounds, including Mound 2, were excavated by the National Park Service in 1964. The elongated Mound 2 is 110 feet long by 60 feet wide and 4 feet high. Excavation revealed that it is actually three mounds in one. Initially, two mounds were built side by side, then both were covered with more earth to create a single, oblong mound. The remains of 41 individuals were found in Mound 2, but there were few accompanying artifacts. Different pottery types found in separate areas of this compound mound indicate that it was constructed in two phases: first during the Late Woodland period and then, after a considerable length of time, during the Mississippian period.

THE LIVING TRACE

107.9 West Florida Boundary

The first Treaty of Paris concluded the struggle for land in the New World between France and Britain, known as the French and Indian War. As a term of the treaty Great Britain received most of the formerly French territory west of the Appalachian Mountains to the Mississippi River. France also ceded West Louisiana to its ally Spain in compensation for western Florida, which Spain yielded to Great Britain. Britain, in turn, created West Florida. In 1764 this spot was the northern boundary of West Florida, marked by a line from the Yazoo and Mississippi Rivers' confluence east to the Chattahoochee River.

✪ TRACE TOP 20

———

NATURAL WONDER

122.0 Cypress Swamp

Crossing the wooden footbridge into this swamp, you enter a watery, quiet world populated primarily by water tupelo and bald cypress. For those who picture the Deep South as a languorous world of Spanish moss and humid mystery, this stop on the Parkway should satisfy your imagination. You can enjoy this easy, flat walking trail in 15 minutes, or you can savor it for much longer, quietly waiting for swamp wildlife (such as herons and alligators) to appear. The tranquility here can be hypnotic if you are unhurried.

Water tupelos (*Nyssa aquatica*) have a bulbous base and will grow to a mature height of 90 feet, with a

A mysterious-looking cypress swamp (milepost 122.0)

spread of 30 feet. Their foliage turns orange-red in the fall, and small, clustered, greenish-white flowers appear in spring with the new leaves. The tree's fruit is one inch long, pear-shaped, and reddish purple in color. The bald cypress (*Taxodium distichum*) will mature to 70 feet in height with a 30-foot spread. Contrary to popular belief, this deciduous conifer can grow in a variety of soils— even dry, compacted ones—but it must have water to germinate, hence its association with swamplands. In swamps the tree forms "knees;" stubby up growths that may help to aerate the plant as well as provide stability in high winds. Bald cypresses have even been known to survive hurricanes.

From her humble beginnings in rural Mississippi, Oprah's legacy has established her as one of the most important figures in popular culture.

—www.Oprah.com

One of the best-known women in the modern world has lived in two places near the Natchez Trace. Oprah Gail Winfrey, generally referred to solely by her first name, was born on January 29, 1954 in a now-gone farmhouse on the rural outskirts of Kosciusko, Mississippi. She started her broadcasting career in Nashville at radio station WVOL when she was still in high school. At the age of 19, she became the youngest person and the first African-American woman to anchor the news at Nashville's WTVF-TV.

Oprah made her acting debut in her 1985 portrayal of Sofia in director Steven Spielberg's *The Color Purple,* a role for which she received both Oscar and Golden Globe nominations. Oprah's daytime talk program, *The Oprah Winfrey Show,* has received so many Emmys (39) that Oprah withdrew it from future competition in 2000. Her mission statement for *The Oprah Winfrey Show* is "to use television to transform people's lives, to make viewers see themselves differently, and to bring happiness and a sense of fulfillment into every home."

NATURAL WONDERS

122.6 River Bend

The Pearl River, named by French explorer Pierre Le Moyne, Sieur d'Iberville, for the many native pearls he found here, is the focus of this scenic area. The river marks a boundary between Mississippi and Louisiana.

NATURAL WONDERS

———

ARCHEOLOGY AND
NATIVE AMERICANS

128.4 Upper Choctaw Boundary

A line of trees that now blends into the surrounding growth marks the dividing line that was established at the Treaty of Doak's Stand on October 20, 1820. As a result of this treaty the Choctaw surrendered one-third of their tribal land—millions of acres—to the United States. Within ten years of signing the treaty, the Choctaw no longer had claim to any land east of the Mississippi. In ten minutes you can easily take the nature trail for a leg stretch and a look at the area's Southern pines.

NATURAL WONDERS

130.9 Yockanookany

"Yockanookany" is a Choctaw word meaning "has been lost." The Yockanookany River is nearby.

By her 40s she found herself at the helm of a multimedia empire that reaches into broadcast and cable television, publishing, the Internet, and film. Oprah is also well known for her charitable giving, especially in the United States and in South Africa.

Time magazine included her in its list of the 100 most influential people of the twentieth century. Oprah was also recognized by the publishing industry for her influential contribution to reading when she received the National Book Foundation's 50th Anniversary Gold Medal in 1999. In 2002, she was honored with the first-ever Bob Hope Humanitarian Award at the 54th Annual Primetime Emmy Awards.

To see the land of Oprah's humble origins, take the MS 35 exit from the Trace, which intersects with MS 12. Buffalo Road, renamed Oprah Winfrey Road, makes a loop off MS 12. Before rejoining MS 12 by traveling on Oprah Winfrey Road you will pass Oprah's first church (now the Buffalo Community Center) and the site of her first public performance, an Easter recitation of "Resurrection of Jesus;" her family cemetery; and the site of her birthplace.

135.5 Robinson Road

KAINTUCK BOATMEN AND THE POSTAL ROAD

Here in central Mississippi some of the first pioneer settlements were made along "Old Robinson Road," which was named for the man who built it under a contract from Congress. Now on the National Register of Historic Places, Robinson Road was begun in 1821 and became a great thoroughfare for travel between Jackson and Columbus.

140.0 Red Dog Road

ARCHEOLOGY AND NATIVE AMERICANS

Named for Choctaw leader or "Minko" Ofahoma (Red Dog) and opened in 1834, the road originated in Canton, Mississippi. Ironically, the opening took place four years after Chief Ofahoma signed the Treaty of Dancing Rabbit Creek, in which the Choctaws agreed to leave their lands here and move to Oklahoma.

145.1 Myrick Creek

NATURAL WONDERS

A pleasant five-to-ten-minute flat walk here can give you a leg stretch. The NPS encourages you to see beavers here, although little evidence of their dams remains.

154.3 Holly Hill

159.7 Kosciusko

Bike-only campground. Please see Chapter Two, "The Nuts and Bolts of Traveling the Trace," (p. 29) for more information.

160.0 Information Center

Kosciusko Chamber of Commerce volunteers provide travel information for the Parkway and local area in a small, comfortable welcome station that offers nature and history exhibits and rest rooms. Exit the Parkway at MS 35 heading west, and the center is on your left up a short, gently sloping driveway.

164.3 Hurricane Creek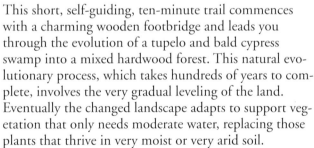

Allow ten minutes to walk this easy trail with a slight elevation gain. You begin by descending into bottom-land along the creek banks, then ascend to where more arid types of trees and plants can survive. A bench at the top will reward you with a place to take a rest before you climb back down. Along this trail you can see how availability of water affects plant life. Self-guiding trail markers help identify plants and different soil conditions.

175.6 Cole Creek

This short, self-guiding, ten-minute trail commences with a charming wooden footbridge and leads you through the evolution of a tupelo and bald cypress swamp into a mixed hardwood forest. This natural evolutionary process, which takes hundreds of years to complete, involves the very gradual leveling of the land. Eventually the changed landscape adapts to support vegetation that only needs moderate water, replacing those plants that thrive in very moist or very arid soil.

176.3 Bethel Mission

For five years, from 1821 until it closed in 1826 as traffic moved away from the Trace, Bethel "House of God" Mission was one of 13 church-based institutions founded by white pioneers. The settlers founded these missions to share their zeal for the Christian gospel with the local Choctaw population. In addition to Bible studies, the missions' agendas often included farming, carpentry, weaving, housekeeping, and the standard academic subjects: reading, writing, and arithmetic. Bethel Mission wasa half mile to the northwest from here.

180.7 French Camp

Louis LeFleur established a stand here in 1812. French Camp Academy, a school catering to the needs of young people who come from broken homes, traces its origins to the school founded here in 1822. Officially chartered in 1885 and once a project of the Presbyterian Church, the school since 1950 has been interdenominational, free of ecclesiastical control. Today it supports about 200 boarders and 85 students from the surrounding area. All students are encouraged to pay tuition, room, and board, but no student is turned down if they cannot do so. French Camp Academy's Rainwater Observatory and Planetarium, not open to Trace travelers, is the largest in the state, with 20 telescopes and other equipment. Sorghum made here in the fall sells quickly to the public.

French Camp has bed-and-breakfast lodging and is a wonderful place to stop for lunch. For more information see Chapter Two, "The Nuts and Bolts of Traveling the Trace" (p. 29)

Split-rail fence at
French Camp
(milepost 180.7)

The Chickasaw lived in northern Mississippi, southwest Tennessee, and northwest Alabama. Their settlements tended to be strung along waterways. There were two divisions of ancient Chickasaw society. One group lived in the woods and served as warriors, while the larger group lived in fortified towns. The largest of these in Mississippi was in the Pontotoc Ridge area and was known as Long Town. It is near present-day Pontotoc. These towns were built with defense in mind, for the Chickasaw had a long-standing reputation as fierce, highly respected warriors.

Like the Choctaw, the Chickasaw were ruled by a "minko." The minko, sometimes called a chief but more properly named a leader, was from the "beloved family" or minko (royal) clan. As with other southeastern tribes, heredity was traced through the female line.

*French Camp Academy, One Fine Place, French Camp, MS 39745; phone (662) 547-6482; **www.frenchcamp.org.***

NPS INFORMATION

193.1 Jeff Busby

Jeff Busby, former public-school teacher, attorney-at-law, and Mississippi congressional representative, is honored at this central location on the Parkway. The honor is fitting considering it was Busby who shepherded a measure through Congress in the mid-1930s "to locate the Natchez Trace as near as practical in its original route and to determine the cost of construction of an appropriate National Parkway."

Jeff Busby the place, is the only stop directly on the Trace that sells gasoline. Other venues are sometimes only five minutes off the once-beaten path, but for those determined to stay the course, Jeff Busby can take on the significance of a mecca. A picnic area, gas station, convenience store with basic wares slightly skewed toward campers, phone, and rest rooms complement the campgrounds. (See Chapter Two, "The Nuts and Bolts of Traveling the Trace" (p. 29) for more camping information.)

A winding, self-guided trail here weaves through a hardwood forest and crests at an overlook that is one of Mississippi's highest points, 603 feet above sea level.

"
a winding, self-guided trail here weaves through a hardwood forest and crests at an overlook that is one of the Mississippi's highest points
"

For nearly 80 years the Chickasaw had to contend with European power struggles in their territory. At the important Battle of Ackia on May 26, 1736 the Chickasaw, supported in part by the British, defeated a French–Choctaw initiative. This decisive battle released France's declining hold west of the Appalachian Mountains, but both the English and the French continued to maneuver for control.

After the defeat of the British during the American Revolution, the native peoples, including the Chickasaw, had to contend with the U.S. government, who eyed hungrily their ancestral lands. As a result of the 1832 Treaty of Pontotoc Creek, in 1837 the Treaty of Doaksville called for the resettlement of the Chickasaws among the Choctaw tribe in Indian Territory (Oklahoma). The Chickasaws were one of the last tribes to move, succumbing both to the pressure to leave their homeland and the promise of an improved existence in Oklahoma.

Exhibits tell the story of America's forests at this crest. Since the trail winds and rises (allow 30 minutes unless you are in "attack mode"), some travelers may wish to drive to the top to enjoy the view.

198.6 Old Trace

THE OLD TRACE

Walking this broad section of the Old Trace you get a distinct understanding of how it meanders across and alongside the present Parkway. Wear closed-toe shoes and probably long pants to protect you from poison ivy and other "itchies," such as chiggers, to enjoy this out-and-back section of the original roadway that leads approximately 500 yards into the woods.

201.3 Ballard Creek

NATURAL WONDERS

This stop features a fairly secluded picnic area with one table.

203.5 Pigeon Roost

NATURAL WONDERS

KAINTUCK BOATMEN
AND THE POSTAL ROAD

Folsom's stand and trading post, operated by Nathaniel and David Folsom, once stood near this point. Millions of passenger pigeons, now extinct, also once roosted here. According to the Smithsonian Institution, at one time this species "constituted 25 to 40 percent of the total bird population of the United States. It is estimated that there were 3 billion to 5 billion passenger pigeons at the time Europeans discovered America."

213.3 Line Creek

While the Natchez Indians lived around the area of present-day Natchez, the Choctaw inhabited the area north and east of Natchez—basically the southern half of what would become Mississippi. The Chickasaw territory included, roughly, northern Mississippi and western Tennessee. This creek was the boundary line between the Choctaw and Chickasaw nations, who were generally not cordial to each other. Legend has it, however, that the two tribes were once one, but that a quarrel between two brothers who were tribal leaders provoked the split into two distinct tribes.

214.5 Dancy

221.4 Old Trace

This approximately ten-foot-wide section of the Old Trace crosses the Parkway. The rough ground is not for those with open-toe shoes. The excursion will take 20 minutes out-and-back and is simply another opportunity to walk in the footsteps of previous Old Trace travelers.

232.4 Bynum Mounds

There are six burial mounds and an associated habitation area at the Bynum site, built during the Middle Woodland period, between BCE 100 and CE 100. The mounds range in height from 5 to 14 feet. The National Park Service excavated five of them in the late 1940s. The two largest mounds, rising like the breasts of a giant woman slumbering just beneath the earth, have been restored for public viewing. Mound A, the southernmost of the two restored mounds, contained the remains of a woman who was buried between two burned oak logs laid at a parallel at the mound's base. She was buried with an ornamental copper spool at each wrist. The cremated traces of two adults and a child were also found here. Mound B, the largest at the site, covered a log-lined crematory pit. An L-shaped row of 29 polished greenstone celts (axe heads) and the cremated and unburned remains of several individuals were found on the ash-covered floor. Other artifacts found laid in ceremonial context include copper spools, 19 chert projectile points from Illinois, and a piece of galena (shiny lead ore). Greenstone, copper, and galena, like the distinctive chert points found here, do not originate in Mississippi. These high-prestige goods, like

A path winds through
the Bynum burial mounds
(milepost 232.4)

those found at the Pharr Mounds, were acquired through long-distance trade networks. Exhibits at the mounds describe the lifestyles of these people.

233.2 Witch Dance

By their nature, legends grow tall out of a grain of truth. Legend has it that at this spot, witches dance, and where they touch down the grass withers and dies. Be that as it may, and given that dead patches of grass are virtually ubiquitous, there is truth to the fact that plenty of souls succumbed to the Trace's hardships and "crossed over" while traveling it. Many, many men, and quite a few women and children who tried to endure its terrain faltered and failed. If you believe in ghosts, you may just feel their presence radiating from this nearly central spot near the Old Trace.

241.4 Chickasaw Agency

From 1801 to 1825 the Chickasaw's agency was located here, serving as headquarters for the Indian agent—a representative of the federal government sent to the American Indian tribes. Natchez Trace historian Ilene Cornwell wrote in her seminal 1984 publication *Travel Guide to the Natchez Trace Parkway:*

. . . one of the most historic sites along the Parkway. Just west of this spot, from 1802 to 1825, was the abode for the United States agents acting as intermediaries to the Chickasaw nation. Efforts of these agents insured peaceful travel through Indian lands; they also performed such thankless tasks as collecting debts, recovering stolen horses, removing trespassers, and capturing fugitives.

Their greatest contribution, however, was probably in fostering peaceful relations between the Native Americans and the white men. In 1812, while he was the Chickasaw Indian agent, James Robertson—founder of Nashville and Father of Middle Tennessee—wrote to his kinsman, Captain John Davis of Big Harpeth in Bellevue: "I am well pleased with my berth, and have had the greatest council that ever was in this nation. . . The Chickasaws profess to be as well pleased with me as I am with them. There cannot be a people more determined to observe peace with the United States than the Chickasaws."

Tishomingo and Piomingo were the ruling Chickasaw leaders, and they counseled repeatedly with the white settlers to maintain peaceful co-existence. The question became a moot one when all Southeastern Indians were removed to Oklahoma along the Trail of Tears in 1838.

NATURAL WONDERS

243.1 Davis Lake

This is the access point to the U.S. Forest Service's recreation and camping area. See Chapter Two, "The Nuts and Bolts of Traveling the Trace," (p. 29) for more information on this facility.

CIVIL WAR
AND OTHER
MILITARY HISTORY

243.3 Hernando de Soto

This Spanish explorer of the Mississippi spent the winter of 1540–1541 near here. According to the Pontotoc Chamber of Commerce, it was in this camp on Christmas Day, 1540 that the first Christian marriage in America was held between Juan Ortiz and Sa-Owana, a Seminole princess held captive by the Spaniards. The event is depicted in a mural in the Pontotoc post office.

It is nearly impossible to study Southern history without coming across the name of Hernando de Soto. Born in Spain, he was the first person from Europe to explore Florida and the southeastern United States. After an expedition in 1524 to present-day Nicaragua where he prospered as a slave trader, he enlisted as an aid of Francisco

Pizarro and headed for Peru in 1531. Here de Soto killed Atahualpa, the Incan leader whom he had befriended. This heinous murder betrayed the faith of de Soto's leader Pizzaro. De Soto returned to Spain in 1536, but still hungry for life in the New World, he was granted rights to Florida and was named governor of Cuba.

De Soto arrived on Florida's west coast on May 30, 1539 with ten ships carrying more than 600 soldiers, priests, and explorers. They spent the next four years searching for gold and silver, exploring the southeast, spreading disease, and behaving with brutality toward the native peoples they encountered: Cherokee, predecessors of the Seminoles, Creeks, Chickasaws, Choctaws, and dozens of smaller, lesser-known tribes. In the end the New World took its own revenge and claimed de Soto with a fever. He died May 21, 1542 and was initially buried on the banks of the Mississippi River that he "discovered." Soon after he was dug up and anchored to the bottom of the Mississippi so that his grave would not be found by the Native Americans.

245.6 Monroe Mission

According to the Pontotoc County Historical Society, Monroe Mission School was the first religious building erected in North Mississippi. The Presbyterian Reverand Thomas C. Stuart, who was known to be "a mighty force in building good relationships" between settlers and the Chickasaw, established the mission in 1821. By 1827, 100 acres were being farmed here and the school had 81 students. Similar to studies at the Bethel Mission south of here, academic study at Monroe Mission for boys included carpentry and agriculture, while the girls were taught spinning and weaving. More than 150 Christian baptisms took place in the church, described as a diminutive room, not over 16 feet by 16 feet.

249.6 Tockshish

Tockshish, Chickasaw for "tree root," or McIntoshville as it was also known, was established by John McIntosh, a British agent, in 1770. McIntoshville was Mississippi's second post office, established in 1801 as a postal relay station between Nashville and Natchez. It took postal riders five days on the trail from Nashville to reach this point, and they still had to travel for another seven to reach Natchez.

Tockshish once had a mission school and church. Such mission schools proved to be training grounds for

"

It is nearly impossible to study Southern history without coming across the name of Hernando de Soto

"

ARCHEOLOGY AND
NATIVE AMERICANS

KAINTUCK BOATMEN
AND THE POSTAL ROAD

young Chickasaws who used the skills they learned here to assume leadership responsibilities after the tribe's subsequent removal to Oklahoma.

251.1 Chickasaw Council House

Like any other nation of people, the Chickasaw needed a central place to conduct the business of government. In the 1820s, the council house at Pontatok became the capital of the Chickasaw nation, where tribal chiefs and leaders met to adopt laws, set policies, and sign treaties. In the Pontotoc Creek Treaty, which was signed here on October 20, 1832, the Chickasaw ceded more than 6 million acres of land to the U.S. Government.

After this treaty a land office was established here in the center of the territory, where, according to the Pontotoc Chamber of Commerce, "for years property changed hands in the amount of $30,000 a day. Thomas MacMackinm the town's founder, purchased a section of land for $1,000m divided it into lots, and sold them within a month for the sum of $80,000."

"

once at the bottom of the sea, limestone deposits over millions of years transformed into very fertile soil

"

251.9 Black Belt Overlook

The overview here highlights an essential cornerstone of the local culture for hundreds of years. "Black Belt" refers to a swath of earth that reaches eastward across nearly all of Alabama, a region known for its rich, black soil excellent for growing crops, especially cotton. Once at the bottom of the sea, limestone deposits over millions of years transformed into very fertile soil. At first a grassland prairie, then a cotton-rich region, this land still supports the local people as a superior pasture for livestock.

TUPELO, MISSISSIPPI

> *They die well who die for faith and home and native land.*
> —From the D.A.R. marker near Tupelo
> that commemorates the Battle of Ackia

The modern city of Tupelo, with nearly 35,000 citizens, stands upon ancient, hallowed ground. From the earliest Indian settlement, the Tupelo area was linked to the outside world via the now-historic Natchez Trace. When Spanish explorer Hernando de Soto passed through this area in 1540, he encountered an established Chickasaw Indian civilization nestled in the wooded hills and valleys. The Chickasaw, who had a reputation as fierce fighters, ultimately drove de Soto westward toward the Mississippi River, the "discovery" for which he is perhaps most famous.

In 1736, at the height of the French and Indian War, a bloody battle erupted near Tupelo between the Chickasaw, supplied in part by the British, and the combined invading forces of the French and the Choctaw Indians. Known as the Battle of Ackia, the engagement left the area in British control and this, in part, contributed to the Crown's eventual domination of North America.

The Civil War also left its mark upon the Tupelo area. The Battle of Tupelo, in mid-1864, pitted Union troops against Confederate cavalry bent on controlling railroad traffic supplying the Union campaign against Atlanta.

Formally incorporated in 1870 and named after the native tupelo gum tree, Tupelo's modern history can be traced to the convergence of the Mobile & Ohio Railroad and the Kansas City, Memphis & Birmingham Railroad companies in 1887. Tupelo was the first city in the nation to provide its citizens with dependable, inexpensive electric power through the Tennessee Valley Authority.

Suggested itineraries for half-day, full-day, and regional tours, as well as tour packages including attractions and events pertaining to the early years of Elvis, are available through the Tupelo Convention and Visitors Bureau.

*Tupelo Convention and Visitors Bureau, P.O. Drawer 47, 399 East Main Street, Tupelo, MS 38802. Phone (662) 841-6521 or (800) 533-0611; **www.tupelo.net.***

Tupelo has several notable attractions, not the least of which is the birthplace of Elvis Presley. One standout is the Tupelo Automobile Museum, which displays more than 100 antique and classic cars. Another worthwhile attraction is the Tupelo Buffalo Park, home to several exotic species and a buffalo herd that includes Tukota, a rare white buffalo who keeps the legendary mystical power of such animals alive. The Sioux Indian tribes believe that a white buffalo is the most sacred of all living animals, and that to see one is great blessing. The buffalo is particularly germane to the Trace story, for these great animals helped in large part to carve the original Trace trails. Great herds would migrate north toward the salt lick and sulfur spring in what is now downtown Nashville. Game of all types was attracted to these trails, which in turn attracted the Native Americans. To see a buffalo here is to observe one of the first and most important of the Trace's travelers.

*Tupelo Buffalo Park and Zoo, 2272 North Coley Road, Tupelo, MS 38803. Phone (662) 844-8709 or (866) 27-bison; fax (662) 844-8592; **www.tupelobuffalopark.com.** $25 for a family including two parents and up to four children. Monday–Thursday, adults $8, children under 12 and senior citizens $6, children under age 1, free. Saturday and Sunday fees are $2 higher per person. Pony rides and guided trail rides also available for a fee. From the Natchez Trace Parkway take MS 45 north (west), also called McCullough*

> "
> Tupelo was the first city in the nation to provide its citizens with dependable, inexpensive electric power through the Tennessee Valley Authority
> "

Boulevard. Turn left on Coley Road. The Tupelo Buffalo Park is almost immediately on your left.

260.0 Elvis Presley's Birthplace and Boyhood Haunts

> *When I was a child, ladies and gentlemen, I was a dreamer. I read comic books, and I was the hero of the comic book. I saw movies, and I was the hero in the movie. So every dream I ever dreamed has come true a hundred times.*
>
> —Elvis's acceptance speech for the 1970 Ten Outstanding Young Men of the Nation Award presented by the Jaycees

Whether or not you are a fan of his music, it's worthwhile to make a pilgrimage to the birthplace of the "Southern version of the Horatio Alger hero" who has sold more records—over a billion globally—than any person on earth. In a quiet Tupelo neighborhood you can go inside the tiny two-room, shotgun-style house built by Elvis's father Vernon. Here Gladys gave birth to Elvis Aaron and his stillborn twin, Jessie Garon. The modesty of the house—especially if you have been to Elvis's opulent Memphis mansion Graceland—is deeply touching. It explains why Elvis, even when his wealth and fame had

The humble birthplace of Elvis Presley in Tupelo, Mississippi (milepost 260.0)

far exceeded his dreams, was also known for his generosity and his identification with working-class people.

The attraction also includes a life-size statue commemorating Elvis at age 13 (when his family moved to Memphis), a small museum, gift shop, and a chapel—a tribute to Elvis's deep attraction to God and gospel.

The birthplace is staffed by knowledgeable employees, who are also loyal Elvis devotees.

Open May to September, Monday–Saturday, 9 a.m.–5:30 p.m. It closes at 5 p.m. in October–April. Sunday year-round, 1–5 p.m. Closed Thanksgiving and Christmas Days. Adult admission: house $2.50, museum $6, combined $7. Children: house $1.50, museum $3, combined $3.50. Phone (662) 841-1245. From the Parkway take MS 6 into Tupelo, where it becomes Main Street. Follow it through town, across railroad tracks. After crossing Veteran's Boulevard take a left on Elvis Presley Drive and follow the signs.

Tupelo also offers a self-guided tour to some of the most significant Elvis-related sites, such as where he bought his first guitar (Tupelo Hardware) and where he hung out (Johnnie's Drive-In). Call (800) 533-0611 for information; or many locations, including the Parkway's Tupelo Visitor Center, can provide you with a map.

259.7 Tupelo National Battlefield

One mile east of the Parkway on MS 6 you can visit the small street-corner park that commemorates the Civil War Battle of Tupelo (also known as the Battle of Harrisburg), which took place on July 14–15, 1864. Major General A.J. Smith, commanding a combined Union force of more than 14,000 men, left LaGrange, Tennessee, on July 5, advancing south. Smith's mission was to insure that the Confederate Major General Nathan Forrest and his cavalry did not raid Major General William T. Sherman's railroad Union lifeline in Middle Tennessee and, thereby, prevent supplies from reaching Sherman in his campaign against Atlanta. Lieutenant General Stephen D. Lee commanded the Confederate forces to attack on the morning of July 14. The Union forces repelled a number of uncoordinated attacks and the Confederates suffered heavy casualties. Short on rations, Smith did not pursue victory but started back to Memphis on July 15. Although Smith was criticized for not destroying Forrest's command, Smith had caused much damage and had fulfilled his mission of securing Sherman's supply lines. Confederate

CIVIL WAR AND OTHER MILITARY HISTORY

"
the Union forces repelled a number of uncoordinated attacks and the Confederates suffered heavy casualties
"

losses included 210 killed, 1,116 wounded, and 47 missing. Union losses amounted to 77 killed, 559 wounded, and 38 missing.

✪ TRACE TOP 20

ARCHEOLOGY AND
NATIVE AMERICANS

261.8 Chickasaw Village Site

"
as you stand on the gentle
rise, try conjuring a
panorama of village life
"

This stop is a Parkway classic if you have a good imagination. Here you can sense the nearly palpable, lingering atmosphere of a long-standing agrarian and hunting culture, a people who frequently needed to defend their homes. Others may see only a typical exhibit sign and some concrete curbs on the ground, marking the outline of Chickasaw seasonal dwellings and a fort. The accompanying exhibits describe daily life and early history here. As you stand on the gentle rise, try conjuring a panorama of village life. A 20-minute out-and-back self-guided, level trail features plants used by the Chickasaw. If you continue the trail out of the woods and walk alongside the road across a field, you will walk a 2-mile trail to Old Town Overlook. You can continue your hike over flat land for another 2 miles for a total of approximately 4.5 miles to reach the Tupelo Visitor Center, headquarters for the Natchez Trace Parkway.

ARCHEOLOGY AND
NATIVE AMERICANS

263.9 Old Town Overlook

The name "Old Town" refers to a Chickasaw village that was here near the "Old Town Creek." "Old Town" in both instances was a pioneer-designated name. For many of these people the Chickasaw language was too challenging, and so they invented names of their own. The Chickasaw name for "Old Town" is lost to history. Old Town Creek is a tributary of the Tombigbee River, first known as the River of the Chickasaw. This area was once the heart of the Chickasaw territory. From here you can hike 2 miles to the Chickasaw Village at milepost 261.8, or you can hike 2 miles in the other direction to the Parkway Visitor Center.

✪ TRACE TOP 20

NATURAL WONDERS

NPS INFORMATION

266.0 Tupelo Visitor Center (Parkway Headquarters)

It is important that you plan your trip so you can spend a little time at the Tupelo Visitor Center, the only Trace information center open year-round.

This can't-miss stop right on the Parkway is a mecca for your mind and body. The NPS staff here can answer your questions and point out ways to make your trip even more enjoyable. You'll find exhibits covering various aspects of Trace life; a free introductory film; brochures on area attractions; and a shop with Trace-related books and gifts. For more mental refreshment, you can stroll on the paved Beech Spring self-guiding trail taking you for about 15–20 minutes through an area of forest regrowth. To the left of the headquarters as you are facing it is a quick access road into Tupelo, along which you will find many motels, a Wal-Mart, and several restaurants.

The Tupelo Visitor Center is open 8 a.m.–5 p.m. daily except Christmas Day.

Brices Cross Roads National Battlefield Site

This Civil War locale can be reached via MS 145 north to MS 370 west. Total detour time off the Trace is about two-and-half hours, allowing one hour for travel and one-and-a-half hours to see the visitor center and the battlefield site.

This battle, also known as Guntown or Tishomingo Creek, has been studied at many war colleges for Confederate Major General Nathan Bedford Forrest's ability to overcome substantial odds. Shelby Foote wrote in *The Civil War: A Narrative, Red River to Appomattox,* "The enemy had a close to two-to-one advantage in men, as well as nearly three times as many guns, but Forrest believed that boldness and the nature of the terrain,

✪ TRACE TOP 20

CIVIL WAR
AND OTHER
MILITARY HISTORY

Brices Cross Roads
Museum near
milepost 266.0

Flags and flowers mark the gravesites of 13 unknown Confederate soldiers (milepost 269.4)

which he knew well, would make up for the numerical odds he faced."

"That devil Forrest," as he was known, was a threat to Union General William Tecumseh Sherman's supply line, vital to his mission to capture the key city of Atlanta. Sherman ordered Union forces at Memphis, Tennessee to march into North Mississippi to find and, ideally, wipe out Forrest and his Confederate cavalry.

On the morning of June 10, 1864, Confederate troops engaged Union forces near Baldwyn, Mississippi along the narrow wooded lanes around Brices Cross Roads. Forrest, who had a near prescient grasp of what the Union commander Brigadier General Samuel D. Sturgis would do, mounted a bloody, day-long battle against a much larger Union army. A long-lasting rain that made wagon-hub-deep mud was followed by high heat, factors that Forrest also used in his rout considered by many to be one of the most decisive victories of the American Civil War. As a result, Forrest acquired a large number of arms and amunition and 1,600 captured men who were on retreat. Counting the captured men, Union troops suffered five times the losses of the Confederates. Yet for the sureness of the victory, Sherman's tactic of engagement had successfully kept Forrest away

from the Union supply lines, and so Sherman's infamous "March to the Sea" was able to continue.

Confederate losses amounted to 96 killed, 386 wounded, 492 missing; Union losses to: 223 killed, 394 wounded, 1,623 missing.

Go first to the Brices Cross Roads Visitor and Interpretive Center, located near the junction of MS 370 and US 45. The center is easily accessed by following the signs. The site itself is located 5 miles west of this center. Heading north on US 45, turn left onto MS 370 to go to the battlefield (open daily from 7 a.m. until sunset) or turn right to go to the Brices Crossroads Visitor and Interpretive Center. This facility offers exhibits and an audio-visual presentation, and is staffed by volunteers. Open Tuesday–Saturday, 9 a.m.–5 p.m.; Sunday, 12:30 p.m.–5 p.m. Closed Monday. Admission, $3 adults, $1 children ages 5–17. For more information call Edwina Carpenter, curator, at (662) 365-3969 or e-mail bcr@dixie-net.com or brices@brice-scrossroads.com.

TUPELO TO THE ALABAMA STATE LINE

269.4 Confederate Gravesites

A five-minute walk on the Old Trace takes you to the graves of 13 unknown Confederate soldiers, whose faintly etched tombstones line the old roadway that once was a prominent final resting place along a busy route. It is unknown whether these men perished from wounds or disease, but their graves speak—mutely yet eloquently—about a chapter in Trace history buried here in the Mississippi soil.

275.2 Dogwood Valley

Stretch your legs for 15 minutes or so as you walk through a large stand of exceptionally mature dogwood trees, some of them more than 100 years old. Blooms on the neighboring younger and smaller species won't guarantee a white, enchanted forest here. Still, the up-and-down loop trail here has beauty in any season.

278.4 Twentymile Bottom Overlook

The low area along the stream is typical of the landscape through which the old Trace passed, offering a strong contrast to the modern conveniences of today's Parkway.

✪ TRACE TOP 20

CIVIL WAR
AND OTHER
MILITARY HISTORY

THE OLD TRACE

NATURAL WONDERS

THE OLD TRACE

283.3 Donivan Slough ⛱ 🚶

You will be welcomed by a single picnic table and, in season, wildflowers on this 15-minute flat, single-track circular trail. It takes you through a dense forest where you can gain an understanding of how occasional flooding influences the variety of plants here. Along the way is a secluded bench for soaking up all the woods have to offer, which could be—along with many wonderful things—mosquito bites at dusk in the late spring, summer, and early fall. Don't forget your bug spray.

286.7 Pharr Mounds

For lovers of archeology, the Pharr Mounds are breathtaking in their scope and mysterious, gentle beauty. Here eight mounds beckon from across a majestic field that the Park Service allows to be harvested for hay. It's tempting to enter the field and approach the earthworks, but to protect the mounds, please refrain. You can easily picture the bustle of life that must have taken place here. This site was occupied during the Late Archaic era, but these burial mounds were built during the Middle Woodland period, between CE 1 and 200. (A roadside sign at the site incorrectly reads 1–1200 AD).

"
cremated and unburned human remains were found in and near these mounds, as were various ceremonial artifacts
"

Ranging in height from 2 to 18 feet, the mounds are distributed over an area of about 90 acres. They comprise one of the largest Middle Woodland ceremonial sites in the southeastern United States. The National Park Service excavated four of the mounds in 1966. The mounds hold various internal features, including fire pits and low, clay platforms. Cremated and unburned human remains were found in and near these features, as were various ceremonial artifacts, including copper spools and other copper objects, decorated ceramic vessels, lumps of galena (shiny lead ore), a sheet of mica, and a greenstone platform pipe. The copper, galena, mica, and greenstone did not originate in Mississippi; they were brought here over long distances through extensive trade networks. Such ritually significant, non-local items typify the Middle Woodland period.

293.2 Tennessee–Tombigbee Waterway and Jamie L. Whitten Bridge ⛱

Here's a spot to contemplate some man-made earth changes while you have a picnic near water hyacinth–laden ponds. To cut the distance between the developing industries of the mid-South and the ocean ports on the Gulf of Mexico by more than 800 miles, in 1946 the United States Congress authorized the U.S. Army Corps of Engineers to plan for a canal between the Tennessee and the Tombigbee Rivers. Such a water connection makes 459 miles navigable between the Gulf of Mexico and Tennessee River. The Tenn–Tom, as is it known, forms a 234-mile-long, 300-feet-wide by 9-feet-deep transportation artery (some call it a ditch) connecting west-central Alabama and northeastern Mississippi. In May 1971 President Nixon turned the first spade of earth, and the Tenn–Tom opened for commercial traffic in January 1985. The most popular commodities shipped by barge are forest products, petroleum by-products, crushed rock, and grains.

Jamie Lloyd Whitten, an U.S. Congressional representative from Mississippi, was born in Cascilla, Mississippi on April 18, 1910. As a school principal he was elected to the Mississippi House of Representatives in 1931. Elected as a Democrat to the Seventy-seventh Congress by special election on November 4, 1941 to fill a vacancy, he subsequently served 54 years. He died in Oxford, Mississippi on September 9, 1995.

There are seven class-A campgrounds near but not adjacent to the Parkway, located on the Tennessee–Tombigbee Waterway. Each provides water and electric hookups, sanitary dump stations, wheelchair-accessible sites and facilities, playgrounds and multiuse courts, as well as convenience. Some have fish-cleaning stations and sewer hookups. Each site has an impact pad, grill, fire ring, picnic table ,and lantern post. Campgrounds on the Tenn–Tom open at 6 a.m. and close at 10 p.m. A number of sites may be reserved through the National Recreation Reservation System, at www.reserveusa.com or by calling (877) 444-6777. Reservations for camping on the Tenn–Tom can be made from March 1 to September 15. First-come, first-served sites are available year-round. Costs for sites range $10–$20 per night. Those with a Golden Age or Golden Access Card pay half price.

293.4 Bay Springs Lake

This is the boat access for Bay Springs Lake and dam, part of the Tenn–Tom waterway managed by the Army Corps of Engineers.

304.5 Tishomingo State Park

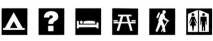

By driving less than five minutes off the Parkway, you can take a side trip to this beautiful state park, a great spot to have a picnic by the lake. The State of Mississippi Department of Wildlife, Fisheries, and Parks says it best:

> *Located in the foothills of the Appalachian Mountains, Tishomingo State Park is steeped in history and scenic beauty. Archeological excavations confirm the presence of Paleo Indians, descendants of the migrants who crossed into America on a land bridge connecting Siberia with Alaska, in the area now encompassed by the park as early as BCE 7000. The park takes its name from the leader of the Chickasaw nation, Chief Tishomingo. The famous Natchez Trace Parkway, the premier highway of the early 1800s and a modern scenic Parkway, runs directly through the park. Today's visitors to Tishomingo State Park discover the same timeless natural beauty that enchanted the Indians centuries ago. Tishomingo offers a unique landscape of massive rock formations and fern-filled crevices found nowhere else in Mississippi. Massive boulders blanketed in moss dot the hillsides, and colorful wildflowers border trails once walked by Native Americans.*

The day-use entrance fees are $2 per vehicle ($0.50 for each person over 4 people), plus $0.50 per person over 4 passengers; motorcycles, $2 per vehicle; pedestrians and bicyclists, $0.50 per person. See Chapter Two, "The Nuts and Bolts of Traveling the Trace" (p. 29), for more information about camping here.

308.4 Cave Spring

The Paleo hunters who used the Bear Creek Mound site (see next entry) probably used this water source. A collapsed underground limestone cavern formed this cave. A short, easy, paved trail takes you to its mouth. Although this was an important water site for thousands of years, for safety reasons the NPS guards against drinking this water or entering the cave.

308.8 Bear Creek Mound

Bear Creek Mound is the oldest prehistoric site on the Trace. At first it was used by migratory hunters as a temporary station, as early as BCE 7000, or roughly 9,000 years ago. It was intermittently occupied for about 8,000 years, or until around CE 1300. Over those millennia the people who used this site shifted their living style from a primitive hunting culture to an efficient hunting and wild-food-gathering economy, and finally to an agricultural society.

The earthwork here was built in several stages between CE 1200 and 1400 for ceremonial or elite residential use during the Mississippian period. Burned daub (mud plaster used in building construction) found on the mound during archeological excavation indicates the former presence of a temple or chief's house. A small, contemporaneous habitation area is located to the south and east of the mound. When acquired by the NPS, the mound had been greatly reduced in height, to about four feet, by plowing. Following excavation in 1965, the mound was restored to its original estimated dimensions of about 8 feet high by 85 feet across the base. Standing on this exact spot you are connected to nearly 10,000 years of human history.

"

over millenia, the people who used this site shifted their living style from a primitive hunting culture to an efficient hunting and wild-food-gathering economy, and finally to an agricultural society

"

308.9 Alabama–Mississippi State Line

ALABAMA MILEPOSTS (313–341.8)

313.0 Bear Creek

NATURAL WONDERS

A lovely park graces the gentle, low bluffs of Bear Creek in this picnic area. With a picturesque view and creek-bed access, this open yet secluded site is a perfect spot to watch children explore.

317.0 Freedom Hills Overlook

NATURAL WONDERS

A paved trail that takes ten minutes to walk at a moderate pace heads up to Alabama's highest point on the Parkway, 800 feet above sea level. Although the ascent is steep, especially at first, two benches provide rest stops along the way. The path is a delight in springtime when it's laced with dogwoods. The view at the top rewards you with a broad vista of the South's green valleys and hills. Since elevation grade along the Trace is generally subtle and most settings look into fields and forests, this vantage point's higher altitude provides a rare sense of overview.

320.3 Buzzard Roost Spring

Exhibits tell the story of Chickasaw leader Levi Colbert, who owned a nearby stand to shelter travelers. The stop at Buzzard Roost Spring is a classic Parkway exercise in imagination, for there is nothing left of Colbert's stand, one of the most famous along the Trace.

Levi was one of several sons of James Logan Colbert, a Scot who immigrated in 1736, quickly fell in with the Chickasaw, and married into the tribe three times. The Chickasaw elevated James's son Levi to a leadership position after he marshaled the boys and old men of the tribe to ambush an invading war party of Muskogee. In addition to the shelter, Levi Colbert's holdings included a gristmill, salt springs, and a plantation powered by slave labor. He had a reputation for intelligence, hospitality,

"

the Chickasaw elevated James's son Levi to a leadership position after he marshaled the boys and old men of the tribe to ambush an invading war party of Muskogee

"

Take a break at a shady glen like this one at Buzzard Roost Spring (milepost 320.3)

and prosperity. Some of his wealth came from compensation he received from the U.S. government during negotiations with the Chickasaw. The Colbert name is prominent in Alabama where the Chickasaw were forced to migrate in 1837 after the 1832 Treaty of Pontotoc.

A short trail leads to the Colbert's stand and Buzzard Roost spring where it is easy to picture how precious the small spring was to Trace travelers. A short descent on steep steps will reveal a quiet haven set in a cool and shady glen, the perfect retreat for a hot summer day.

To reach Shiloh National Military Park at milepost 320, take AL 72 west toward Iuca. In Iuca, at the intersection of AL 25/57, turn right, heading north. After approximately 15 miles, Pickwick Landing State Park will be on your right. Take AL 57 to the left, then turn right on AL 142 to reach the park.

Shiloh has a tragic stillness nearly unique among southern Civil War battlegrounds. One of the more poignant settings is Bloody Pond where wounded soldiers (both Union and Confederate) came to cleanse their wounds, or take a last drink before dying. It is named Bloody Pond, because the water turned blood-red from all the wounded and dying soldiers that littered its banks.

The Park was established in 1894 to preserve this scene of the first major battle, also known as Pittsburg Landing, in the Western theater of the Civil War. The two-day battle, April 6 and 7, 1862, involved about 65,000 Union and 44,000 Confederate troops. This battle resulted in nearly 24,000 killed, wounded, and missing. It proved to be a decisive victory for the federal forces when they advanced on and seized control of the Confederate railway system at Corinth, Mississippi. The battlefield covers about 4,000 acres, so as you visit you can think of roughly six men per acre that were killed, maimed, or written off as missing. Within the battlefield boundaries are the Shiloh National Cemetery along with the well-preserved, prehistoric Indian mounds, a historic landmark. The park is located in Hardin County, on the west bank of the Tennessee River, and about 9 miles south of Savannah, Tennessee.

The Shiloh National Military Park Visitor Center is open year-round, 8 a.m.–5 p.m. Admission for a family in a single private vehicle is $5 for 7 days; individual fee, $3 for 7 days. Take AL 72 west toward Iuca. At the intersection of AL 25 and AL 57 turn right, heading north. After approximately 15 miles, Pickwick Landing State Park will

CIVIL WAR
AND OTHER
MILITARY HISTORY

"

the battlefield covers about 4,000 acres, so as you visit you can think of roughly six men per acre that were killed, maimed, or written off as missing

"

*Tawny and unsubdued, an Indian among rivers, the old
Tennessee threw back man's improvements in his face and
went its own way.*

—Donald Davidson in
The Tennessee: The Old River

Another son of the Scotsman James Logan Colbert and a
Chickasaw woman, George Colbert operated a stand and his
ferry here. When President Jefferson sent General James
Wilkinson to improve the Trace, George Colbert served as a
negotiator for the Chickasaw. Colbert, who always dressed as a
white man and was reportedly shrewd and well spoken,
appears to have been a cunning man who cared more for his
own self-interest than he did for the Chickasaw Nation. In
return for delivering permission to develop the road, Colbert
was granted the rights to operate a stand and a ferry here to
ford the Tennessee River.

Reports that he charged Andrew Jackson $75,000 to ferry
his army across the river are probably greatly exaggerated.
Another account claimed he made $20,000 from Jackson's
troops, but Jackson's account book indicated payment of only
a few hundred dollars. Still Colbert monopolized the vital
river-crossing trade. His basic charges, high by his own admission, were $0.50 for a foot passenger, and $1 for a horse and
rider. In his defense, Colbert claimed that he fed and ferried
many sick and destitute travelers for free.

*be on your right. Take AL 57 to the left, then turn right on
AL 142 to reach the park.*

✪ TRACE TOP 20
———
KAINTUCK BOATMEN
AND THE POSTAL ROAD
———
NPS INFORMATION

THE LIVING TRACE

327.3 Colbert Ferry

The main attraction at Colbert Ferry is the Tennessee
River, since the ferry station is submerged. The ranger
station is rarely staffed, but there are the amenities of
rest rooms, swimming, fishing, boat launch, and a bike-
only campground. Don't miss the expansive picnic area
along the river, reached by taking the road that circles
down, around, and behind the ranger station.

328.6–327.8 John Coffee Memorial Bridge
This 0.8-mile span crosses Pickwick Lake formed by
Pickwick Landing Dam on the Tennessee River. This
modern bridge is named for Andrew Jackson's political
ally and military crony, General John Coffee, who

The Tennessee River here bears little relation to the river that faced the Trace's travelers. It is now a chain of lakes linked together by the hubris of TVA dams and locks built in the 1930s and 1940s. It is not the "tawny and unsubdued" river of the pre-dam years.

With his poet's eye, Donald Davidson wrote in *The Tennessee: The Old River*:

> One of the chief peculiarities of the old Tennessee is that, of all the great rivers east of the Mississippi, it has been least friendly to civilization. Until the advent of the Tennessee Valley Authority, it defied every human attempt at conquest. It could be used, but only at great hazard and on terms forbidding to commerce and industry. So it remained a wild river, cherishing its wildness while civilization rushed across it or away from it.

The river that Donaldson wrote about, the river foot travelers had to cross, was the Trace's single greatest obstacle. The river then was substantially lower than today's fattened, lazy lake now spanned by a bridge. The pre-TVA river could present itself as a 600-mile roaring mess of mud, logs, and current. To give you some idea of the former river's power, TVA now claims that its flood-control efforts prevent an estimated $177 million in damage each year in the Tennessee valley.

served with Jackson at the Battle of New Orleans in 1815. Jackson selected Coffee to be the U.S. negotiator with the Choctaw at Dancing Rabbit Creek in 1830 and with the Chickasaw at Pontotoc Creek in 1832. Coffee got the job done to Jackson's satisfaction. The upshot of both treaties was the surrender of all native Indian lands.

Jackson's attitude toward Native Americans was patently paternalistic. In 1818 he wrote to Isaac Shelby:

> . . if the present spirit of the Indians are [sic] not checked, by some act of the government shewing [sic] them their real state of dependence, in a short time, no cession of land will be obtained from them—The Colberts (presumably George and Levi) say, they will part with their lands for the price the United States gets for theirs. These are high-toned sentiments for an Indian and they must be taught to know that they do not posses [sic] sovereignty, with the right of domain.

328.7 Lauderdale

This small, fairly exposed picnic area is on the northern side of the Tennessee River. The picnic area at Colbert's Ferry, less than five minutes south, is much more scenic and restful.

330.2 Rock Spring

A self-guided trail along Colbert Creek. If you love water, or want a truly refreshing break, don't miss Rock Spring. It has the quality of an enchanted forest with changing scenery at every turn, and useful information on trail markers about the surrounding animal and plant life. The NPS map recommends 20 minutes for this nature walk. Usually the Service's estimates are generous by five to ten minutes, but Rock Spring has such a lovely, secluded variety of environments you may want to linger much longer.

An easy single-track loop trail, with a rise at the back, invites you to begin the hike, fording the spring-fed stream by treading on large chunks of dressed stone. These stones also make a great spot to sit in the sun and feel its warmth while you refresh your feet in the creek.

The trail meanders along the streambed and, within five minutes, a bench under a shade tree invites you to "set a spell." With a mix of hardwoods behind you and open wetland in front of you, you might see beavers or herons, if you are lucky.

The trail continues back to the shady source of the spring, which flows from beneath a small overhang. The large rock at this site no doubt gave the place its name, and it's another good spot to rest, or even picnic. If you want to feast closer to your vehicle, there's a table at the trailhead. Many stops on the Trace don't fully remove you from the busyness of the blacktop, but Rock Springs' plush privacy takes you a world away.

> "
> the quality of an enchanted forest with changing scenery at every turn, and useful information on trail markers about the surrounding animal and plant life
> "

341.8 Tennessee–Alabama State Line

TENNESSEE MILEPOSTS (343.5–444)

343.5 Cypress Creek

An expansive, shady picnic area with easy access to the broad, sun-dappled creek where rock hounds can enjoy a quiet break and children can splash in the stream.

346.2 Holly

NATURAL WONDERS

An open field removed from the Parkway offers high shade, several picnic tables, and easy access to the creek.

350.5 Sunken Trace

THE OLD TRACE

The original Trace was always a work in progress. It was not always a single path, and certainly it was not always clear which way to proceed. The three sections of the original road here show how the route was relocated to avoid mud holes. The paths converge about 40 yards to the right of the paved parking area. They contrast the rough terrain the Trace's foot-weary had to trek with the Parkway's smooth surface.

352.9 McGlamery's Stand

KAINTUCK BOATMEN AND THE POSTAL ROAD

A nearby village still bears the name of the stand that was founded here by a man named John McGlamery in 1849, nearly 40 years after Trace travel peaked in the 1810s. The stand was in business for about 12 years, but closed at the advent of the Civil War in 1861.

363.0 Sweetwater Branch

NATURAL WONDERS

An initial steep descent becomes a gently rolling out-and-back trail along the Sweetwater Branch creek. One bench along the way and one at trail's end provide chances to soak in the water and enjoy the flora and bird presence here. Several easy access points permit wading in the tumbled-rock creek bottom. The final bench can be a good destination for a shady picnic. The round-trip should take about 30 minutes if you don't linger, but you'll probably want to, especially if there are wildflowers in bloom.

364.5 Glenrock Branch

NATURAL WONDERS

Set below the Parkway, this pull-off is a natural shady haven for family picnics. Adults can keep an eye on children while they explore this dappled glen set alongside the curve of a creek framed by a high limestone-cutaway bluff. A 0.6-mile trail leads to Upper Glenrock, another good place to picnic.

367.3 Dogwood Mud Hole

THE LIVING TRACE

There isn't anything to "see" here, but this marker helps to remind you of what the Trace was like in periods of heavy rain. An often-impassable mud hole lies nearly a mile to the south.

✪ TRACE TOP 20

THE OLD TRACE

375.8 Old Trace Drive

Note: Not for travel trailers.

This 2.5-mile road follows the original Trace route and has one-way traffic heading north. Traveling about 20 miles per hour is suggested, especially to enjoy the three overlooks with pretty views of the countryside. The pace and isolation here can help your mind and body gear down to the rhythm of the old road. Given the light traffic here, hikers may enjoy an out-and-back walk, or they can return to their cars via the Parkway for approximately 1 mile for a total loop hike of 3.5–4 miles.

NATURAL WONDERS

377.8 Jacks Branch

Another cool, shady drop below the level of the Parkway, this picnic spot has steps down from the roadway. It does have rest rooms, but it is not as easily accessible or as scenic as the Glenrock Branch Picnic area roughly 12 miles south at milepost 364.5.

THE LIVING TRACE

381.8 Napier Mine

This open pit was worked in the nineteenth century to supply ore for the tools the settlers needed. Shellfish deposited here throughout this part of Tennessee more than 400 million years ago have transformed into limestone layers containing phosphate, an important fertilizer at least since the 1860s.

KAINTUCK BOATMEN
AND THE POSTAL ROAD

THE OLD TRACE

382.8 Metal Ford

If you're looking for a good old-fashioned swimming hole, Metal Ford is your stop. With picnic tables and a grassy, open field, it gives you all the ingredients for a daylong summer adventure. Metal Ford takes its name for the metal-like, smooth-stoned Buffalo River bottom. With a gentle current that varies between ankle-to-chest deep, this is a nostalgic place to let your cares be washed downstream. In July swimmers report an excellent water temperature and easy maneuvering on the rock bottom. A short trail to the right as you face the river will take you to an old millrace, a river channel whose current fed Steele's Iron Works to produce primitive pig iron in the early 1800s. This stop also features picnic tables.

John McLish, a Chickasaw mixed blood, operated a
nearby stand during some of the Trace's prime years,
between 1812 and 1822, capitalizing on this spot where
Trace travelers forded the Buffalo River.

385.9 Meriwether Lewis

This stop is rich with possibilities. Within its 300 acres
you can learn about a murder mystery, hike part of the
Old Trace, picnic in a secluded cul de sac, and explore
the beauty of both the ridge and hollow along Little
Swan Creek. The campground here is one of the three
along the Parkway run by the NPS, including Jeff Busby

✪ TRACE TOP 20

THE LIVING TRACE

NPS INFORMATION

*His courage was undaunted; His Firmness and Perseverance
Yielded to Nothing but Impossibilities; a Rigid Disciplinar-
ian, yet Tender as a Father of Those Committed to his
Charge; Honest, Disinterested, Liberal, with a Sound
Understanding and a Scrupulous Fidelity to Truth.*

—inscription on Meriwether Lewis's grave,
written by Thomas Jefferson

An explorer, soldier, presidential personal secretary, governor,
woodsman, and writer, Meriwether Lewis accomplished
much in his 35 years. He volunteered at the age of 20 for the
Virginia militia and with some speed rose to the rank of captain. During this time Thomas Jefferson noticed Lewis's capa-
bilities and appointed him to be his personal secretary in
1801. While Lewis lived at Monticello he had access to Jefferson's extensive library, thus furthering his well-rounded education and enhancing his writing skills. Bored with
administrative work, Lewis jumped at the chance to lead an
expedition to explore the Louisiana Purchase—a mission that
Jefferson fully backed. Lewis chose William Clark, a close
friend from his years of military service, to be his co-com-
mander. In the spring of 1804 the "Corps of Discovery" set off
to find an all-water route to the Pacific Ocean.

While the adventurous rewards of the Lewis and Clark
Expedition are well known, or at least well imagined, the
Corps made perhaps an equal contribution to scientific knowl-
edge by returning with new plants and animals, as well as sci-

at milepost 193.1 and Rocky Springs at milepost 54.8.
Like the others it is free. (For more information on
camping, see Chapter Two, "The Nuts and Bolts of
Traveling the Trace" (p. 29)). Several miles of hiking
trails, in addition to the Old Trace section, offer a close
look at young oak-hickory woods laced with dogwoods.

The primary attraction here is the grave of Meriwether Lewis, whose death remains a mystery. Lewis, co-
commander of the famous Lewis and Clark expedition,
was traveling from St. Louis to Washington, D.C. He
was either shot to death or committed suicide on the
night of October 10, 1809 at Grinder's Stand, the first
inn north of the Chickasaw nation, operated by whites.
(A log cabin to suggest the inn has exhibits on the life of
Lewis.) Mrs. Grinder, wife of the innkeeper, reported
that Lewis was restless throughout the evening, and
when the two shots rang out she was afraid to leave her
room. The next morning, October 11, Lewis, who had a

"
Meriwether Lewis's death
remains a mystery. He was
either shot to death or committed suicide
"

entific observations of the land and sociological observations about the Native Americans they encountered. These reflections were preserved in detailed journals.

In 1807 Jefferson rewarded Lewis's efforts with the governorship of the Upper Louisiana Territory. Headquartered in St. Louis, his administration was plagued by problems of debt, bad land speculation, disorganization, numerous complaints, and the comparatively sedentary life of politics still chafed against his more active nature. He also had problems with his love life. Jefferson noted in 1813 with the benefit of hindsight that during this time Lewis was subject to "hypochondriac affections." In September 1809 Lewis set out for Washington, D.C. to discuss financial matters. He opted for the more direct overland route, disembarking at what is now Memphis, Tennessee. This choice put him on the Natchez Trace.

His tragic and violent death on the Trace remains a mystery. Perhaps his fragile mental state prompted him to take his own life, or perhaps he was murdered, as were many other travelers on the Trace. The innkeepers themselves may have done the deed. A great deal of interest still swirls around his fate, and some history buffs have even argued for exhuming his body (nearly 200 years after his death) to determine the cause of his demise. The known truth about Meriwether Lewis, however, is that he was an extraordinarily talented young man whose 15 years of service to his country had a profound and positive impact on a young America.

history of depression, was found barely alive with wounds to his head and chest. He died that day, at age 35, and was buried along the Trace. In 1848 the State of Tennessee erected the monument you see today over his gravesite, a broken shaft symbolizing the untimely conclusion to his life.

386.6 English Camp Branch

NATURAL WONDERS

Down a grassy slope you can enjoy the picnic table situated right beside a gentle waterfall.

391.9 Fall Hollow

NATURAL WONDERS

It takes less than a five-minute walk on this short, paved trail to arrive at a viewing platform where you can admire a small jewel of a waterfall with a 20-foot drop. As Lori Finley says in her book *Traveling the Natchez*

Trace, "No excuses on this one. Granny can manage this easy path, even with her Sunday pumps still on." Those who continue on will find an enchanting open-air maze of paths, bridges, overlooks, and more waterfalls that run even in mid-July.

NATURAL WONDERS

392.5 Swan View Overlook

Swan Creek, which also passes through the Meriwether Lewis campgrounds, is the inspiration for this beautiful spot. The creek was either named for an early 1800s post rider known as "Old Man Swaney," or "Swan," or for the swans that reportedly once lived here.

THE OLD TRACE

397.4 Old Trace

Until the early 1800s the Chickasaw nation's land extended from north-central Mississippi and northern Alabama into middle and western Tennessee. Historian Ronald N. Satz recounted the tribe's loss of this land in *Tennessee's Indian Peoples: From White Contact to Removal, 1540–1840:*

> *Between 1805 and 1818 General Andrew Jackson and other treaty commissioners used threats, economic coercion, and bribery to extinguish Indian title to nearly 20 million acres of land . . . In 1805, the Chickasaws ceded to the United States a section of their domain northeast of the Tennessee River, composed mostly of a large tract of land in Middle Tennessee, in exchange for a cancellation of a $12,000 debt. Despite the economic coercion that produced this cession, the Chickasaws reaffirmed their loyalty to the United States during the War of 1812 by providing fighting men for the American army in the campaign against the Creek Red Sticks. One year after the battle of New Orleans, General Jackson "rewarded" them for their assistance: in 1816, Jackson and his fellow commissioners saw to it that the Chickasaws lost tribal title to all land on the northeast side of the Tennessee River, including a large southwestern portion of Middle Tennessee. After the Treaty of 1816, the only land remaining to the Chickasaws within the Tennessee region was in West Tennessee. Two years later, this too would belong to the United States.*

The Trace here was the boundary line of Chickasaw lands ceded to the United States in 1805 and 1816.

KAINTUCK BOATMEN
AND THE POSTAL ROAD
———
THE OLD TRACE

400.2 Sheboss Place

A stand once serving travelers on the Trace stood here. By agreement the stands that were on Chickasaw grounds existed by permission of the tribe, and the operators often had a direct link to the Chickasaw. The legend of Sheboss Place is that a full-blooded Chickasaw man who spoke very little English, married a white woman, and together they operated this rest stop. When Trace travelers arrived and began to converse and ask questions, the Chickasaw man would point to his wife and say simply, "Sheboss." True or not, it makes a wonderful story.

401.4 Tobacco Farm

The primary interpretive element here is an old tobacco barn that still has some leaves suspended from the rafters. Other exhibits explain tobacco growing. A one-way, 2-mile drive along the Old Trace begins here. At first fairly rough and rutted, the path finally becomes a version of old pavement as it slopes you gently down the ridge to join the Parkway. Suitable for cars with regular and high clearance, this section is probably not for RVs or cars with very low ground clearance. Hikers will especially enjoy the basically flat, slightly downhill grade that is made even more pleasant by the valley overview through the fairly mature forest.

THE LIVING TRACE

————

THE OLD TRACE

403.7 Old Trace

This 2,000-foot section of the original Trace dead-ends into the woods. The trail begins with a very short paved section, but quickly becomes less "civilized." Although the NPS keeps it cut, you may come upon it in somewhat rough condition. This trail is basically flat but is not a place for open-toe shoes. If the grass is high be sure to scrub your legs and feet at first opportunity to rid yourself of chiggers. (See Chapter Two, "The Nuts and Bolts of Traveling the Trace,"(p. 29) to learn more about the harmful or aggravating creatures you might encounter along the Parkway.)

THE OLD TRACE

404.7 Jackson Falls

It's almost impossible to know if Andrew Jackson ever saw this waterfall named for him, although he did have a rather involved and literally romantic history with the Natchez Trace. Although a visit to see fully this milepost requires a 900-foot descent and then, of course, return ascent, visitors invariably say it was worth the effort.

✪ TRACE TOP 20

————

NATURAL WONDERS

For land, for love, and for war, Andrew Jackson traveled the Natchez Trace at least five times. Probably his first trip on the old trail was in 1790 when he returned a runaway slave from the Spanish territory. Historians think that on this trip he purchased some land about 25 miles north of Natchez near Springfield, the mansion where he later married the love of his life, Rachel Donelson Robards. After escorting his wife-to-be to Natchez via flatboat, Jackson returned home via the Trace. After he and Rachel married in August 1791, they also returned home by way of the old road.

Jackson's military affiliation with the Trace began when as Major General he commanded his "Tennessee Volunteers" to proceed south to prevent British occupation of West Florida in the War of 1812. After his troops were stalled in Natchez for a month, Jackson received a letter from the Secretary of War indicating that plans had changed and that Jackson was to disband his men where they were and let them fend for themselves to return home. Jackson resisted this order. He was determined to take his men—some of them sick—home, where they could be compensated for their service and properly discharged. On this march Jackson earned the nickname "Old Hickory," the implication being that he was as tough as

When you pull into the parking area, take the trail to the right. A half-mile trail to Bakers Bluff veers to the left. You can walk in the woods to Bakers Bluff and then return by roadside, if you prefer.

The at-most ten-minute hike to Jackson Falls is paved, bridged, and stepped down to the falls themselves, which makes it fairly easy. Here you find a large, circular limestone gorge that has a flow even in August—usually a dry month in Tennessee. This current feeds into the Duck River. At the bottom a bench welcomes you, as does a cooler atmosphere and many flat rocks for poking about to feed, as one mother put it, "creek fever." Rest rooms and a picnic table are at the trail top.

NATURAL WONDERS

405.1 Bakers Bluff Overlook

This stop can also be reached by a roughly half-mile hike from Jackson Falls. The single-track trail is hilly and, like on most wooded paths along the Parkway, you'll want to watch out for poison ivy. At Bakers Bluff overview you gaze down upon a working family farm in a picturesque setting. Exhibits here draw your attention to how good conservation practices work with the systems of the earth.

hickory wood. In 1815 Jackson again marched home on the Trace after defeating the British army at the Battle of New Orleans. This victory poised him to become the seventh president of the United States.

Andrew Jackson was a complicated man. American-born of Scots-Irish heritage, with flaming red hair, and a temper to match, he was orphaned at age 14. He succeeded at law, in the military, in land speculation, in duels, and in politics. By almost every account, his dealing with Native Americans, including Seminole, Creek, Choctaw, Cherokee, and Chickasaw peoples, was by turns barbarous, underhanded, coercive, demeaning, and cruel, yet he reared several Indian orphans at his home in Nashville, called the Hermitage.

Jackson's greatest triumph—his strong, important, and controversial presidency—was marred by the death of his beloved wife Rachel who died three months before he took office in 1829. A champion of "the common man," he is also remembered as a dominant early-nineteenth-century personality, spawning Jacksonian Democracy as well as "The Age of Jackson." He was, in sum, much like the Natchez Trace he knew: demanding, unforgiving, difficult, rewarding, and eventually offering a mixed legacy of both trouble and promise.

407.7 Gordon House and Ferry Site

The strong Gordon spirit still lingers around this 1818 house, home of John and Dolly Cross. The Gordon House and Mount Locust (milepost 15.5) are the only two surviving structures from the Old Trace's early 1800s era. The Gordons built this brick home, the remainder of a plantation that once encompassed more than 1,500 surrounding acres. After first living in Nashville, the couple moved here to run the ferry across the Duck River established in 1801 by troops as part of the new federal road, the Natchez Trace. This section of the Trace road ran from the Tennessee Valley Divide (milepost 423.9) southward to Colbert's Ferry on the Tennessee River. John Colbert was a Native American fighter whose health deteriorated partly due to his military exploits under Andrew Jackson. Unfortunately, he lived in this new house less than a year before he died in 1819. Faced with a declining ferry business due to dwindling traffic on the Trace, Dolly Gordon managed the farm until she died. Although the home is closed now, the NPS acquired it in 1977 and has plans to make it an interpretive station.

✪ TRACE TOP 20

———

THE LIVING TRACE

———

KAINTUCK BOATMEN AND THE POSTAL ROAD

"

this brick home is the remainder of a plantation that once encompassed more than 1,500 surrounding acres

"

One woman who made a home beside the trace was Dorothy (Dolly) Cross Gordon. Born in Virginia in 1779, Dolly came to Nashville as a child. Her father, Richard, was a merchant and their family lived in a stone house on Broad Street. With her dark hair and eyes, Dolly was proud of her descent from Pocahontas. When she was introduced to Captain John Gordon, she knew fate had taken a hand in her life. Gordon was exactly 15 years older and the two shared the same birthday, July 15, which later became their wedding day.

In 1812, the Gordons moved to Hickman County and began to operate a ferry across the Duck River. John was often away, leaving Dolly alone with their ten children. People came from far and near to see the Gordon's two-story home, the first brick one in 30 miles. John Gordon always ended his letters with "I am, dear Dolly, your affectionate husband." These happy times came to an end in 1819, when, four months after the birth of daughter Louisa, John Gordon died.

For 40 years, Dolly Gordon ran her plantation alone. Characterized by a kind disposition, a positive nature, and respected

To walk a mile, stroll down the bank toward Fattybread Creek. If the footbridge is out, make your own way across to the field on the other side, and rest on the bench for a spell. Continue up a hill on this section of the Old Trace and follow it toward the Duck River. You will reach a level spot by the water that was the waiting grounds for the ferry, long since swept away by the cold currents of winter storms, but in operation until the bridge was built in 1896. A narrow path can take you closer to the Duck. As you go, think of how many times the enduring Dolly Cross Gordon made this same trek.

NATURAL WONDERS

411.8 Water Valley Overlook

A lone picnic table sits high atop a rolling hillside. Although the commanding view is marginally marred by TVA power lines, this is still a very pleasant spot with an isolated, yet open, feeling.

NATURAL WONDERS

423.9 Tennessee Valley Divide

When Tennessee joined the Union in 1796, this watershed was the boundary between the United States to the north and the Chickasaw nation to the south. This physiographic feature is part of the Highland Rim that surrounds the middle Tennessee basin.

for her upright principles and business judgment, she managed her children's education and her financial affairs with equal care and success. Mrs. Gordon owned slaves, one of whom, Lewis, served as her foreman. He and his wife, Silvy, operated their own small business, making and selling ginger cakes and cider. The nursemaid, Lydia, was taught to read from the family Bible along with the children.

Dolly Gordon remained, in the words of her granddaughter, "astonishingly active to the day of her death." Horseback was her choice of transportation, and she went wherever she cared to go, fording the Duck River and visiting her grandchildren at Columbia, 15 miles away. There was a carriage for very harsh weather, but Dolly preferred her "good roan."

—Adapted from "Women of the Natchez Trace"
by Carol Farrar Kaplan, published in the March–April
1999 issue of *Tennessee Conservationist*

425.4 Burns Branch

NATURAL WONDERS

This stop has two primary functions. It is part of the Garrison Creek horse path and has the necessary hitching posts to prove it. (See Chapter Three, "The Many Ways to Travel the Trace," (p. 29) for more information on horseback riding.) Those not on horseback, however, will find it to be a memorable picnic spot, with four tables generously spaced alongside a placid, cooling creek bed.

426.3 Old Trace

THE OLD TRACE

The U.S. Army stationed at Garrison Creek cleared this section of the "Natchez Road" in 1802–1803 and continued clearing southward with the consent of the Chickasaw nation. You can take an easy 2-mile hike to Garrison Creek under a mature forest canopy that can be glorious in the fall. If you are just getting on the Trace and heading south, you might want to read the interpretive exhibits in the center grassy area of this pulloff, as they give you a quick overview of the Trace story.

427.6 Garrison Creek

CIVIL WAR
AND OTHER
MILITARY HISTORY

Named for a nearby 1802–1803 U.S. Army post, this area is a trailhead for horseback riders and hikers. It's a nice picnic spot along the waterway, with plenty of room for horse trailers to maneuver. There's also a sign map that shows the Garrison Creek hiking and horse trail loop. (See Chapter Three, "The Many Ways to Travel the Trace," (p. 47) for more information on this trail.)

THE LIVING TRACE

428.9 Leiper's Fork

To enjoy a quaint, quirky small town, exit the Parkway at TN 46. Leiper's Fork was established in 1785 as Benton-town, named after Thomas Hart Benton, who later became a United States Senator in Missouri for 30 years. You can see the location of the Benton home, but another house has since been built atop the Benton foundation.

"

enjoy a quaint, quirky small town . . . the surrounding area is home to several of Nashville's recording artists, including the Judds

"

The community's name was changed when the Bentons left for Missouri. Settlers from Hillsboro, North Carolina who moved to the area changed the name to Hillsboro. Early in the twentieth century, the name was changed to Leiper's Fork, after nearby Leiper's Creek.

The surrounding area is home to several of Nashville's recording artists, including the Judds. You can sometimes catch live music at Green's Grocery and as well at a regular "Writer's Night" on Tuesdays at the Country Boy Restaurant. Go to the Leiper's Web site, **www.williamson-tn.org/commun/leipers.htm,** and click on "Bigfoot Sighting" for a little extra fun.

✪ TRACE TOP 20

———

THE LIVING TRACE

438.0 Highway 96 Double-Arch Bridge

"Creating Bridges as Art" proclaims the Web sitre for the Figg Engineering Group of Tallahassee, Florida. Underneath this bold aesthetic claim is an image of the Natchez Trace Parkway's double-arch bridge, spanning a tranquil valley and TN 96. It's easy to see why the company parades this structure: it is breathtakingly beautiful from just about every angle. The view from the bridge at 155 feet above the valley floor, which you can access from the milepost pull-off on the north side of the span, is a very good one. It is essential, however, that you pull off the Parkway at the exit for TN 96 on the southern side of the bridge to appreciate its soaring, elegant construction. You can easily turn around and get right back on the Trace.

This is the nation's first arch bridge constructed with segments of concrete, and it spans a hefty 1,648 feet. The bridge's arches are designed to support the deck without evenly spaced spandrel columns, resulting in an unencumbered appearance. In all, 196 superstructure and 122 arch segments were used to produce it at a cost of $11.3 million—considered reasonable for such a stunningly successful solution. Highly acclaimed, the bridge has been honored with 13 design awards, including the very prestigious Presidential Award for Design Excellence from the National Endowment for the Arts in 1995.

444.0 Northern Terminus Intersection with TN 100

Although the National Park Service (NPS) has hopes for a welcoming interpretive center here, at present just another of the Parkway's key bridges transports you to and from the Natchez Trace's "ribbon of time." If you are exiting the Parkway it will feed you to the right onto TN 100 toward Nashville. Or you can travel on the bridge to cross over TN 100 for a sweep left that will send you west toward Fairview, Tennessee. If you are entering the Parkway from Nashville, go under the bridge, bear to your right, open your eyes and mind, and let the Natchez Trace Parkway time capsule work its magic.

NASHVILLE

The first settlers in what is now known as Nashville were Indians of the Mississippian culture, who lived in the area around CE 1000–1400. They raised corn, made great earthen mounds, painted beautiful pottery—and then mysteriously disappeared. Other Indians, the Cherokee, Chicksaw and Shawnee, followed and used the area as a hunting ground.

The first white men to come to the area were French fur traders who established a trading post around 1717. The first settlement, however, was not established until 1779. It was then, on the banks of the Cumberland near the center of present downtown Nashville, that a band of pioneers led by Englishman James Robertson cleared the land and built a log stockade. This was Fort Nashborough, named in honor of General Francis Nash, who won acclaim in the Revolutionary War. John Donelson and some 60 families followed in April 1780, to settle the new community that was then a part of North Carolina. In 1784 the community's name was changed from Nashborough to Nashville.

Tennessee became the 16th state in 1796, and Nashville was made its permanent capital in 1843. By 1860 Nashville was a prosperous city, soon to be devastated by the Civil War. Because of its strategic location

If you look at a modern-day map of Nashville you can see that the old major artery roads resemble the spokes of a wheel that once came together at what is today's Tennessee Bicentennial Capitol Mall, a 19-acre urban park just north of the State Capitol. Animals made these original roads. Fossils indicate that, starting 2.5 million years ago, Pleistocene mammals converged here, including giant camels, elephant-like mastodons, wild horses, deer, ox-sized ground sloths, native American pigs called peccaries, and saber-toothed tigers. More recently, powerful and plentiful herds of buffalo trod the same paths. They all came in search of the salty sulfur spring, to imbibe the remains of an ancient sea that covered West and Middle Tennessee beginning 570 million years ago. At the Mall you can visit the site of this ancient spring, which is arguably what brought the Natchez Trace and its Parkway into existence. Ask a ranger at the welcome center near the Capitol end of the

on the river and the railroad, the city was occupied by Federal troops for three years. The Battle of Nashville, fought in December 1864, was the last major offensive launched by the Confederate Army in the western theater of the war.

In the decades following the war, Nashville once again experienced a growth in population, business and industry, and education. Another area of growth was in country music, which has grown to the extent that Nashville today is known as Music City, USA. Under its present Metropolitan Charter, which became effective April 1, 1963, Nashville and Davidson County have a single government with its authority encompassing more than a half-million people and 533 square miles.

Nashville has many splendid attractions. One that pertains obliquely to the Trace story is The Hermitage. It was the home of Andrew Jackson, who frequently traveled the old road and earned his nickname "Old Hickory" on it. The Hermitage, which has undergone a major restoration, has returned the house and grounds to how it appeared during Jackson's retirement years from 1837 to 1845. Here you can see how a former president lived, as well as the humble origins of his large plantation home.

The Hermitage: Home of President Andrew Jackson, 4580 Rachel's Lane, Nashville, TN 37076, phone (615) 889-2941; **www.thehermitage.com.** *Admission: $12 adults; $11 seniors 62 and older and students ages 13–18;*

> " country music has grown to the extent that Nashville today is known as Music City, U.S.A. "

Mall, or on the Mall, face the State Capitol on the hill. From the street below the Capitol, James Robertson Parkway, come down about one third of the length of the Mall, and then head left toward the Cumberland River along a winding concrete-paved path. A freshwater fountain now marks the general spot of the powerful magnet that helped to make the Natchez Trace, but underneath the pavement the historic, salty, sulfur blend still swirls beneath your feet on it way to the river.

The Bicentennial Capitol Mall offers many outdoor historical and cultural exhibits on Tennessee. Fountains at the River Wall offer refreshment, especially to children, on hot days. The Mall is free and open to the public year-round, closing at dark. It is located at the foot of the State Capitol between James Robertson Parkway, Jefferson Street, and 6th and 7th Avenues. Exits from the Interstates are marked Bicentennial Mall.
www.state.tn.us/environment/parks/parks/Bicentennial

$5 children ages 6–12; free for children under age 6. $34 family rate for 2 adults and 2 children. Daily 9 a.m.–5 p.m. Closed Thanksgiving, Christmas, and the third week in January. The Hermitage is located 12 miles east of downtown Nashville and is accessible from I-40, Exit 221A (The Hermitage exit). From I-65 North the Hermitage is accessible from Exit 92 (Old Hickory Boulevard South exit).

(On opposite page)
Brilliant red and yellow wildflowers in bloom line the route of the Natchez Trace Parkway

Resources

● ●

The references below were helpful in writing this book, and I am indebted to the authors for their contributions. I refer these materials to you for your enjoyment, as many are quite interesting and easy to read.

AUDIO

Natchez Trace Parkway: A Road Through the Wilderness, Eddie and Frank Thomas, in cooperation with the Natchez Trace Parkway and the National Park Service, Iuka, Mississippi: Thomasfilms, Inc. 1994. Eight-and-a-half hours of commentary and some music on cassette organized by milepost markers for north-to-south and south-to-north driving travelers can be purchased at **www.amazon.com** or at the Tupelo Visitor Center. The interspersed music is sometimes cloying, but audio learners will enjoy this colloquial, fact-filled tour that's worth the $39.95 price tag.

BOOKS

Coates, Robert M. *The Outlaw Years.* Gretna, Louisiana: Pelican Publishing Company, 2002. First published in 1930, this is a delicious if somewhat antiquated-in-style biographical rendering of some of the Trace's more gruesome, unscrupulous characters.

Cornwell, Ilene J. *Travel Guide to the Natchez Trace Parkway between Natchez, Mississippi and Nashville, Tennessee.* Nashville: Southern Resources Unlimited, 1984. Out-of-print, but a wonderful compendium chock-full of facts organized by milepost marker—if you can find it. Cornwell was one of the first authors in recent years to champion the Trace.

Crutchfield, James A. *The Natchez Trace: A Pictorial History.* Nashville: Rutledge Hill Press, 2000. First published in 1985, this is a great armchair-history browse with black-and-white images of the Trace sites, vintage illustrations, and maps.

Daniels, Jonathan. *The Devil's Backbone: The Story of the Natchez Trace.* Gretna, Louisiana: Pelican Publishing Company, 1998. A thorough and elegantly written history, beginning with the de Soto period.

Davis, William C. *A Way Through the Wilderness: The Natchez Trace and the Civilization of the Old Southwest.* New York: HarperCollins, 1995. The most scholarly of these titles, this is still a smooth read.

Finley, Lori, *Traveling the Natchez Trace.* Winston–Salem: John F. Blair, 1997. A solid touring guide by milepost marker organized from north to south, with unique dining and lodging options, including bed-and-breakfast recommendations.

Natchez Trace Parkway Survey. Pace, Florida: Trent's Prints, 2002. The report from the Secretary of the Interior of February 26, 1940 that prepared the way for the modern Parkway. This surprisingly good read, with maps for those deeply interested in the Trace's development, can be found at the Tupelo Visitor Center's gift shop.

Molloy, Johnny. *60 Hikes within 60 Miles: Nashville.* Birmingham: Menasha Ridge Press, 2002. Five Tennessee Parkway hikes are described in great detail.

Summerlin, Cathy and Veron. *Traveling the Trace: A Complete Tour Guide to the Historic Natchez Trace from*

Nashville to Natchez. Nashville: Rutledge Hill Press, 1995. The Trace from north to south and packed with a lot of nearby destinations, including shopping, accommodations, and festivals along the way.

Timme, Stephen L. and Caleb C. K. Timme. *Wildflowers of the Natchez Trace.* Jackson: University Press of Mississippi, 2000. A handsome book that profiles and includes illustrations of 100 species, including listings of their locations along the Parkway.

Wanner, Glen. *Bicycling the Natchez Trace: A Guide to the Natchez Trace Parkway and Nearby Scenic Routes.* Nashville: Pennywell Press, 2002. The bible for cyclists on the Trace Parkway.

PAMPHLETS

"Natchez Trace Parkway Teacher's Information Packet," prepared by the Natchez Trace Visitor Center staff. Tupelo: National Park Service, April 2002. A treasure trove on various topics.

Phelps, Dawson A. "The Natchez Trace: Indian Trail to Parkway." In *Tennessee Historical Quarterly,* vol. XXI, No. 3, September, 1962. Reprinted by Eastern National in 1998 and 2003. This trustworthy, clear historical overview by the premier Natchez Trace authority of his day can be purchased at the Tupelo Visitor Center for $1.95.

INTERNET

Alabama State Parks
www.dcnr.state.al.us/parks/state_parks_index_1a.html

Arcadian Outdoor Guide to Canoeing, Kayaking, and Rafting Outfitters in Alabama
www.thetent.com/arcadia/ms

Arcadian Outdoor Guide to Canoeing, Kayaking, and Rafting Outfitters in Mississippi
www.thetent.com/arcadia/ms

Arcadian Outdoor Guide to Canoeing, Kayaking, and Rafting Outfitters in Tennessee
www.thetent.com/arcadia/tn

Bed-and-breakfast lodging locator including areas near the Trace
www.bbonline.com

Bicycling the Trace in a simplified overview
www.byways.org/browse/byways/2285/description/?
   page=Bike%2FPed

Brices Crossroads Visitor and Interpretive Center
www.bricescrossroads.com

**Buffalo Peak outfitters: links to outdoor resources,
   including paddling opportunities**
www.buffalopeak.net/outdoorlinks.html

The Carriage House Restaurant at Stanton Hall in Natchez
www.discoverourtown.com/webs/natchezms/
   carriagehouse

Chickasaw nation information site
www.mnsu.edu/emuseum/cultural/northamerica/
   chickasaw.html

Choctaw nation official site
www.choctawnation.com

Council House Café at French Camp
www.frenchcamp.org/councilhouse.html

Craftsman's Guild of Mississippi
www.mscraftsmensguild.org

Elvis Presley's official site
www.elvis.com

Elvis Presley's first home
www.elvispresleybirthplace.com

Indian Mounds of Mississippi
www.cr.nps.gov/nr/travel/mounds/index.htm

Loveless Café and Motel
www.lovelesscafe.com

**Mississippi Daughters of the American Revolution's
   inscriptions on Trace markers**
www.telapex.com/~dar/trace.htm

Mississippi history
www.mshistory.K12.ms.us/features

**Mississippi, history of native inhabitants and
   European settlement**
www.factmonster.com/ce6/us/A0859677.html

Mississippi, Jackson Convention and Visitor's Bureau
www.visitjackson.com

Mississippi, Kosciusko Chamber of Commerce
www.kosciuskotourism.com

Mississippi, Natchez official site
www.cityofnatchez.com

Mississippi, Pontotoc County Chamber of Commerce
www.pontotocchamber.com/historysub.htm

Mississippi, Pontotoc County history
www.rootsweb.com/~mspontot/tour.htm

Mississippi, Ridgeland official site
www.ridgelandms.org/history.htm

Mississippi River facts
www.nps.gov/miss/features/factoids

Mississippi State Parks
www.mdwfp.com/scrWildlife/ParkSummary.asp

Mississippi tourism
http://visitmississippi.org

Mississippi tourism along the Trace in Natchez, Ridgeland/ Jackson, Kosciusko, and Tupelo
www.scenictrace.com

Mississippi, Tupelo tourism
www.tupelo.net/about-tupelo

Mississippi, Vicksburg Convention and Tourism Bureau
www.vicksburgcvb.org

Mississippian Mound Builders information site
www.mnsu.edu/emuseum/cultural/northamerica/ chickasaw.html

"Natchez Trace (The): An Historical Parkway," a 1939 Regional Review article by Malcolm Gardner, Acting Superintendent, Natchez Trace Parkway Project, www.cr.nps.gov/history/online_books/regional_review/ vol2-4d1.jpg

Natchez Trace Parkway National Park Service
www.nps.gov/natr

Natchez Trace Parkway maps
www.nps.gov/natr/pphtml/maps.html

Natchez Trace Parkway nearby attractions with an emphasis on Civil War battlefields and military parks
www.nps.gov/natr/pphtml/attractions.html

Natchez Trace Parkway National Park Service maps that include hiking and horse trails
(not always clearly indicated)
www.nps.gov/natt/pphtml/maps.html

Natchez Trace research collection holdings at the University of Southern Mississippi
www.lib.usm.edu/~archives/m249.htm

Natchez Trace wildflowers
(organized by color and bloom period)
www.nps.gov/natr/wildflowerwatch.htm

NRRS (National Recreation Reservation Service) for USDA Forest Service, Army Corps of Engineers, National Park Service, Bureau of Land Management and Bureau of Reclamation outdoor recreation facilities and activities
www.reserveusa.com/jsp/homepage.jsp?goto=/home/about.html

Oprah Winfrey's official site
www.oprah.com

Pleasure Walking Horse Association of Tennessee schedule of group rides, some on the Trace
www.pwhat.com/trail.htm

Ross Barnett Reservoir official site with camping and more information
www.rossbarnettreservoir.org/

Shiloh National Military Park   www.nps.gov/shil

Tennessee, Hillsboro–Leiper's Fork
www.williamson-tn.org/commun/leipers.htm

Tennessee, Nashville Convention and Visitors Bureau
www.nashvillecvb.com

Tennessee State Parks
www.state.tn.us/environment/parks

Tombigbee National Forest Davis Lake Recreation Area
www.southernregion.fs.fed.us/mississippi/tombigbee/recreation/davis_lake

Treaty of Doak's Stand
mshistory.k12.ms.us/features/feature14/doaks_1.html

Tupelo, Battle of
www2.cr.nps.gov/abpp/battles/ms015.htm

Tupelo Buffalo Park and Zoo, home to the largest herd east of the Mississippi River
www.tupelobuffalopark.com

Vicksburg National Military Park
www.nps.gov/vick/index.htm

Windsor Ruins
www.southpoint.com/states/ms/windsor.htm

Appendixes

• •

APPENDIX ONE:

ACCOMMODATIONS WITHIN A 15-MINUTE BICYCLE RIDE OF THE PARKWAY

Listed South to North

Natchez, MS (milepost 0)

Numerous motels and bed-and-breakfast accommodations are available here. For a listing, contact: Natchez Convention and Visitors Bureau, 422 Main Street, Natchez, MS 39120; (601) 446-6345 or (800) 647-6724; fax (601) 442-0814. The Mississippi Welcome Center is located at 370 Sargent S. Prentiss Drive, just south of its intersection with US 84 and US 98. To contact the center, call (601) 442-5849.

Lorman, MS (milepost 27)

Rosswood Plantation MS 552, East Lorman, MS 39096; (800) 533-5889 or (601) 437-4215; fax (601) 437-6888. Directions: From Parkway milepost 30, take MS 552 east 1 mile to US 61, then south (right) 1 mile on US 61 to Lorman, then east (left) 2.5 miles on MS 552 to Rosswood. Grocery items are available at the Lorman Country Store.

Port Gibson, MS (milepost 38)

Oak Square (bed-and-breakfast) 1207 Church Street, Port Gibson, MS 39150; (800) 729-0240 or (601) 437-4350. Gibson's Landing

1002 Church Street, Port Gibson, MS 39150; (601) 437-3432. Directions: For northbound bikers, from Parkway milepost 37.7 take US 61 north into Port Gibson. Oak Square is approximately 2 miles on the right and Gibson's Landing is 2.2 miles on the left. For southbound bikers, from milepost 41.1 take MS 18 west 1.3 miles into Port Gibson, then south (left) on US 61. Gibson's Landing is approximately 0.8 miles on the right and Oak Square is 1 mile on the left. There are restaurants in town.

Grand Gulf Inn US 61, North Port Gibson, MS 39150; (601) 437-8811. Directions: At Parkway milepost 37.7, take US 61 north into Port Gibson; the motel is approximately 3 miles on the left. Or, from Parkway milepost 41.1, take MS 18 west 1.3 miles into Port Gibson, then north (right) on US 61; the motel is approximately one-quarter mile on the left. There are restaurants in town.

Clinton, MS (milepost 87)

Clinton Inn 400 US 80, East Clinton, MS 39056; (601) 924-5313. Directions: Motel is in Clinton one block from Interstate 20 west, and is available from either I-20 Exits 34 or 35. The motel is approximately 2 miles southeast (right) from the Parkway at milepost 87.2 (the exit at I-20 west). Bicyclists can exit the Parkway at milepost 84.7 onto Norrel Road and go south approximately 700 feet to Raymond. Clinton Road, east (left) 2.9 miles to I-20, then south (right) 1 mile on US 80 east to the motel. There is a restaurant at the motel. Note: As there is no direct access off the Parkway to Norrell Road, bicyclists only are permitted–using the utmost care–to walk their bicycles down the embankment.

Jackson MS (milepost 95)

Best Western Jackson 5035 I-55, North Jackson, MS 39206; (601) 982-1011.

Hampton Inn 465 Briarwood Drive (Briarwood Dr at I-55 north), Jackson, MS 39206; (601) 956-3611. Directions: At Parkway milepost 102.4, adjacent to the Mississippi Crafts Center, take access road to US 51, then south (left) on US 51.

Motel 6 6145 I-55 north (on I-55 west frontage road), Jackson, MS 39213; (601) 956-8848.

Red Roof Inn 828 MS 51 North (I-55 and County Line Road), Ridgeland, MS 39157; (601) 956-7707

*All motels listed above are approximately 3 to 3.5 miles south through Ridgeland and are adjacent to I-55 north. Many more motels are located in Jackson, but the ones listed here are most convenient to the Parkway. Numerous restaurants are also nearby.

Kosciusko MS (milepost 160)

Days Inn MS 35 South Bypass, Kosciusko, MS 39090; (601) 289-2271. Directions: At Parkway milepost 160, take access road to MS 5. Motels and restaurants are to the right.

Parkway Inn–Best Western MS 35 South Bypass, Kosciusko, MS 39090; (601) 289-6252.

Red Bud Inn 121 North Wells Street, Kosciusko, MS 39090; (601) 289-5086. Directions: Exit Parkway at milepost 160 at Chamber of Commerce Visitor Center. Cross MS 35 onto Huntington Street. Go north on Huntington and turn left onto Washington Street. The Inn is at the dead end of Washington Street.

French Camp, MS (milepost 181)

French Camp Academy (bed-and-breakfast) French Camp, MS 39745; (601) 547-6835 or 547-6657. Directions: At Parkway milepost 180.8, go to the log cabin adjacent to the Parkway and ask directions, or stay on the main street leading into French Camp, turning left onto the road just past the post office and crafts store. There is a restaurant in town.

Mathiston, MS (milepost 204)

Mathiston Motel US 82, Mathiston, MS 39752; (601) 263-8219. Directions: At Parkway milepost 204.3, take US 82 east (right) into Mathiston. Motel is approximately 1.3 miles from the Parkway. There is a restaurant in town.

Houston, MS (milepost 229)

Holiday Terrace Motel MS 8, East Houston, MS 38851, (601) 456-2522; **Southwind Guest House**, 335 South Jackson, Houston, MS 38851, (601) 456-4376, after 2 p.m. (601) 456-2349. Directions: At Parkway milepost 229.7, take MS 8 west 4 miles into Houston. Restaurants in town.

Tupelo, MS (milepost 260)

Comfort Inn 1190 North Ciloster, Tupelo, MS 38801; (601) 842-5100 or (800) 228-5150.

Days Inn 1015 North Gloster, Tupelo, MS 38801; (601) 842-0088 or (800) 325-2525.

Econo Lodge of Tupelo US 78 East (McCullough Boulevard) (located behind the Executive Inn), Tupelo, MS 38801; (601) 844-1904 or (800) 424-4777.

Economy Inn 708 North Gloster, Tupelo, MS 38801; (601) 842-1213; Executive Inn, 1011 North Gloster, Tupelo, MS 38801; (601) 841-2222 or (800) 533-3220.

Hampton Inn 1516 McCullough Boulevard, Tupelo, MS 38801; (601) 840-8300.

Holiday Inn Express 923 North Gloster, Tulpelo, MS 38801; (601) 842-8811 (800) 465-4329.

Mockingbird Inn Bed & Breakfast 305 North Gloster, Tupelo, MS 38801; (601) 841-0286.

Passport Inn 401 North Gloster, Tupelo, MS 38801; (601) 812-1961.

Ramada Inn 854 North Gloster, Tupelo, MS 38801; (601) 844-4111 or (800) 228-2828.

Trace Inn 3400 West Main, Tupelo, MS 38801; (601) 842-3555. Directions: The motel is located on MS 6 adjacent to the Parkway at milepost 260.1. There is a restaurant at the motel, and others east on West Main Street.

Travelers Motel 915 North Gloster, Tupelo, MS 38801; (601) 844-2221.

Village Inn Motel 1013 North Gloster, Tupelo, MS 38801; (601) 842-4903. Directions: At Parkway milepost 262.3, take McCullough Boulevard (old US 78) south 1 mile to the junction of US 45 Business. An alternate route is at Parkway milepost 266, to take US 45 Business south 4.2 miles toward Tupelo. There are restaurants at motels or nearby. This area features four-lane divided highways and two-lane highways with heavy traffic and narrow shoulders.

Campground at Barnes Crossing Route 1, Box 28A, Tupelo, MS 38801; (601) 844-6063. Directions: At Parkway milepost 266, take access leg adjacent to the Tupelo Visitor Center to US 45 Business. Campground entrance is 0.3 miles toward Tupelo.

Tombigbee State Park Route 2, Box 336, East Tupelo, MS 38801; (601) 842-7669. Directions: At Parkway milepost 263.6, take US 78 east 3 miles toward Tupelo and Birmingham. Exit onto North Canal Street and follow park signs. Park will be 2.5 miles east of MS 6, a total of 10.8 miles from the Parkway exit; or at Parkway milepost 266.1, take US 45 Business south 0.8 mile to Barnes Crossing Road (first stoplight), left 0.3 miles on Barnes Crossing Road to the US 45 Bypass, right on the bypass 1.6 miles to US 78, east on US 78 for 1.5 miles toward Birmingham. Exit onto North Canal Street and follow park signs. Park will be 2.5 miles east of MS 6 south, a total of 12 miles from the Parkway exit. Furnished cabins are available, but reservations are recommended, especially from Memorial Day to Labor Day. A full hookup campground is also located here. A restaurant is located at the entrance road to the park on MS 6 south. *Note:* The Elvis Presley Birthplace Home and Memorial Chapel are located one block east from North Canal Street—signing is prominent.

Belmont, MS (milepost 297)

Belmont Motel P.O. Box 140, Belmont, MS 38827; (601) 454-7948. Directions: At Parkway milepost 297, exit and travel east on MS 4 to MS 25. Then travel south on MS 25 to downtown Belmont.

Tishomingo, MS (milepost 304)

Tishomingo State Park P.O. Box 880, Tishomingo, MS 38873; (601) 438-6914. Directions: At Parkway milepost 303.9, take entrance road into park. At main park road, go right 3.5 miles to the headquarters area. Furnished cabins are available, but reservations are recommended, especially from Memorial Day to Labor Day. A full hookup campground is also here. Restaurants are located near the park entrance on MS 25, or at Dennis or Tishomingo, 4 miles either direction from the park entrance on MS 25.

Iuka, MS (milepost 320)

Key West Inn 199 County Road 180, Iuka, MS 38852; (601) 423-9221. Directions: At Parkway exit 320, travel 15 miles west on US 72 to Iuka.

Napier Road Exit, TN (milepost 380.8)

Natchez Trace Wilderness Preserve (privately-owned recreational time-share facility) 1363 Napier Road, Hohenwald, TN 38462; (615) 796-3211. Directions: At Parkway milepost 380.8, exit onto Napier Road, following it around and under the Parkway overpass to the "Trading Post," a gas and grocery store with the preserve office just beyond. Overnight camping for bicyclists is sometimes allowed (inquire at the preserve office).

Hohenwald, TN (milepost 386)

Shadow Acres Motel 699 Centerville Highway, Hohenwald, TN 38462; (615) 796-2201. Directions: At Parkway milepost 385.9, take TN 20 north toward Hohenwald for 7 miles; or at Parkway milepost 391.4, take US 412 (formerly TN 99) west toward Hohenwald for 8 miles. The motel is located approximately 1 mile north of the downtown area on TN 48 North. Restaurants are located in town.

Swan View Motel 1240 Columbia Highway, Hohenwald, TN 38462; (615) 796-4745. Directions: At Parkway milepost 391.1, take US 412 (formerly TN 99) west toward Hohenwald. The motel is 1 mile on the left; restaurant is adjacent.

Waynesboro, TN (milepost 370)

Natchez Trace Motel Route 6, Box 414, Lawrenceburg, TN 38464; (615) 722-3010. Directions: At Parkway milepost 369.9 or 370.1, take US 64 west toward Waynesboro. Motel is located one-half mile on the right from the Parkway. A restaurant is adjacent.

Hampshire, TN (milepost 391)

Ridgetop (bed-and-breakfast) P.O. Box 193, Hampshire, TN 38461; (615) 285-2777. The owners of Ridgetop also offer a free reservation service for bed-and-breakfast accommodations along the Parkway. Call (800) 377-2770. They specialize in bike-trip assistance. Directions: At Parkway milepost 391.1, take US 412 east toward Columbia for approximately 4.4 miles. Ridgetop is 0.3 miles to the left on a private road.

Duck River, TN (milepost 408)

McEwen Farm Log Cabin (bed-and-breakfast) P.O. Box 97, Duck River, TN 38454; (615) 583-2378. Directions: At Parkway milepost 407.8, take TN 50 west toward Centerville for 2.1 miles, then turn right onto Bratton Lane. McEwen Farm is one-half on the right on Bratton Lane.

Leipers Fork, TN (milepost 428)

Namaste Acres–Natchez Trace (bed-and-breakfast) 5436 Leipers Creek Road, Franklin, TN 37064; (615) 791-0333. Directions: Exit Parkway at milepost 429.

Note: The listings below are an approximately 3–60 minute ride from the Parkway.

Columbia, TN

Columbia is located approximately 27 miles east of the Parkway, and at the present time provides an avenue of travel between the Parkway and I-65. Three motels, one bed-and-breakfast, and numerous restaurants are located in Columbia. For a listing, write: Columbia Chamber of Commerce, 9 Hunter-Matthews Building, Public Square, Columbia, TN 38401; (615) 388-2155.

Franklin, TN (milepost 436)

Franklin is located on TN 96, approximately 6 miles east of Leipers Creek Road/Hillsboro Road. This scenic two-lane road presently is one connection between the Parkway and US 31, US 431, and I-65 into Nashville.

Best Western Inn I-65 and TN 96, Franklin, TN 37064l; (615) 790-0570 or (800) 25l-3200. **Holiday Inn** I-65 and TN 96, Franklin, TN 37064; (615) 794-7591. Directions: Both motels are located 3 miles east of Franklin on TN 96 adjacent to I-65. Restaurants are at the motels and nearby.

Nashville, TN

Numerous motel accommodations are available in the Nashville area. For a listing write: Nashville Area Chamber of Commerce, 161 Fourth Avenue North, Nashville, TN 37219; (615) 259-4700.

Note: This list of current lodging accommodations adjacent or reasonably handy to the Natchez Trace Parkway was provided by the NPS. They make no claims regarding the completeness of the listing or the quality of services provided by the establishments.

APPENDIX TWO:

CHAMBERS OF COMMERCE FOR TOWNS WITHIN APPROXIMATELY 20 MILES OF THE PARKWAY

Alabama

Florence–Lauderdale Tourism
  1 High Tower Place
  Florence, AL 35630
  (256) 740-4141 or (888) 356-8687
  www.flo-tour.org

Muscle Shoals, Sheffield, Tuscumbia
  Colbert County Tourism and Convention Bureau
  P.O. Box 740425
  Tuscumbia, AL 35674
  (256)383-0783 or (800)344-0783
  www.colbertcountytourism.org

Mississippi

Booneville
  100 West Church Street
  P.O. Box 927

Booneville, MS 38829
(662) 728-4130 or (800) 300-9302

Brandon
Rankin County Chamber of Commerce
101 Service Drive
P.O. Box 428
Brandon, MS 39043
(601) 825-2268
www.rankinchamber.com

Calhoun City
102 South Monroe Street
P.O. Box 161
Calhoun City, MS 38916
(662) 628-6990

Carthage
Leake County Chamber of Commerce
103 North Pearle Street
P.O. Box 209
Carthage, MS 39051
(601) 267-9231
www.leakems.com

Clinton
Clinton Chamber of Commerce
100 East Leake Street
Clinton, MS 39056
(601) 924-5912
www.clintonms.org

Corinth
The Alliance
810 Tate Street
P.O. Box 1089
Corinth, MS 38835
(662) 287-5269 or (877) 347-0545
www.corinth.ms

French Camp
French Camp Welcome Center
Highway 413 South
French Camp, MS 39745
(662) 547-6113
www.frenchcamp.org

Fulton
Itawamba County Chamber of Commerce
107 West Wiygul Street
P.O. Box 577
Fulton, MS 38843
(662) 862-4571
www.itawamba.com/fulton.htm

Houston

Chickasaw Development Foundation
P.O. Box 505
Houston, MS 38851
(662) 456-2321
www.houstonms.org

Iuka

Tishomingo County Development Foundation
203 East Quitman Street
Iuka, MS 38852
(662) 423-0051 or (800) 386-4373
www.tishomingo.org

Jackson

Jackson Convention and Visitors Bureau
P.O. Box 1450
Jackson, MS 39215
(601) 960-1891 or (800) 354-7695
www.visitjackson.com

Kosciusko

Kosciusko-Attala Chamber of Commerce
124 North Jackson
P.O. Box 696
Kosciusko, MS 39090
(662) 289-2981
www.kopower.com/coc/coc.htm

Madison

P.O. Box 544
Madison, MS 39130
(601) 856-7060
www.madison.ms.us

Natchez

Natchez Convention and Visitors Bureau
640 South Canal Street, Box C
Natchez, MS 39120
(601) 446-6345 or (800) 647-6724
www.cityofnatchez.com

Okolona

219 Main Street
P.O. Box 446
Okolona, MS 38860
(662) 447-5913
www.okolona.org

Pontotoc

Pontotoc County Chamber of Commerce
81 South Main Street
P.O. Box 530

Pontotoc, MS 38863
(662) 489-5042
www.pontotoc.net

Port Gibson
Port Gibson–Claiborne County Chamber of Commerce
P.O. Box 491
Port Gibson, MS 39150
(601) 437-4351
www.portgibson.org

Raymond
Raymond Chamber of Commerce
PO Box 1162
Raymond, MS 39154
(601) 857-8942 or (888) 543-1863

Ridgeland
304 MS 51
P.O. Box 194
Ridgeland, MS 39158
(601) 856-0600
www.ridgelandchamber.com

Starkville
322 University Drive
Starkville, MS 39759
(662) 323-5783
www.starkville.org

Tupelo
Tupelo Convention and Visitors Bureau
P.O. Drawer 47
Tupelo, MS 38802
(662) 841-6521 or (800) 533-0611
http://tupelo.net

Verona
194 Main Street
P.O. Box 416
Verona, MS 38879
(662) 566-2211

Vicksburg
Vicksburg–Warren Chamber of Commerce
2020 Mission 66
P.O. Box 709
Vicksburg, MS 39181
(601) 636-1012
www.vicksburg.org

Tennessee
Columbia/Maury County
106 West Sixth Street
P.O. Box 1076

Columbia, TN 38402
(931) 388-2155 or (800) 205-9641
www.mauryalliance.com

Fairview
P.O. Box 711
Fairview, TN 37062
(615) 799-9290
www.fairview-tn.com

Franklin/Williamson County
109 Second Avenue South #137
P.O. Box 156
Franklin, TN 37065
(615) 794-1225 or (800) 356-3445
www.williamson-franklinchamber.com

Hohenwald
Lewis County Chamber of Commerce
112 East Main Street
P.O. Box 182
Hohenwald, TN 38462
(931) 796-4084
www.visitlewis.com

Lawrenceburg
Lawrence County Chamber of Commerce
1609 North Locust Avenue
P.O. Box 86
Lawrenceburg, TN 38464
(931) 762-4911
www.chamberofcommerce.lawrence.tn.us

Nashville
211 Commerce Street, Suite 100
Nashville, TN 37201
(615) 259-4700 or (615) 657-6910
www.nashvillechamber.com

Savannah
Hardin County Chamber of Commerce
818 Main Street
Savannah, TN 38372
(731) 925-2363
www.hardinchamber.org

Waynesboro
Wayne County Chamber of Commerce
P.O. Box 675
Waynesboro, TN 38485
(931) 722-9022
www.waynecountychamber.org

APPENDIX THREE:
CAMPGROUNDS NEAR THE NATCHEZ TRACE PARKWAY

Departments of Tourism General Information

Alabama	(800) 252-2262
Mississippi	(800) 927-6378
Tennessee	(800) 462-8366

State Parks General Information

Alabama	(800) ALA-PARK	(800) 252-7275
Mississippi	(800) GO-PARKS	(800) 467-2757
Tennessee	(888) TN-PARKS	(888) 867-2757

*Also visit **www.reserveamerica.com** for campsite reservations.*

Listed from South to North

RIVERVIEW RV PARK (milepost 0.0)

(318) 336-1400   Private campground. Electric, water, dump station, sewer hookups, pool, fee area. 155 sites, numerous pull-throughs and back-ins. Cross over MS River bridge into LA 131—0.7 miles.

TRACEWAY (milepost 8.1)

(601) 445-8278   Private campground. Electric, water, sewer hookups, dump station, showers, fee area. 21 sites, 8 pull-throughs and 13 back-ins. 0.1 mile south of the Parkway on US 61.

NATCHEZ STATE PARK (milepost 8.1)

(601) 442-2658   Electric, water, sewer hookups, dump station, showers, fee area. 50 sites, 2 pull-throughs and 48 back-ins. 1 mile East of Parkway on US 61.

GRAND GULF STATE PARK (milepost 41.1)

(601) 437-5911   Electric, water, sewer hookups, dump station, showers, laundry facilities, fee area. 42 sites, 2 pull-throughs and 40 back-ins. 4 miles north of Port Gibson on US 61, turn west onto Grand Gulf Road and ride 6 miles.

ROCKY SPRINGS (milepost 54.8)

No phone   A National Park Service-run campground. No reservations; free of charge. Drinking water, hiking. 22 sites. On the Parkway.

TIMBER LAKE (milepost 103.4)

(800) 388-2267 or **(601) 992-9100**   Private campground. Electric, water, sewer hookups, showers, fee area. 108 sites, back-ins only. Turn east on Spillway Road, cross dam, go 4.5 miles.

JEFF BUSBY (milepost 193.1)

A National Park Service-run campground. No reservations, free of charge. Groceries and food, gas, drinking water, hiking; 18 sites. On the Parkway.

RED HILLS RV PARK (milepost 195.2)

No phone   Private campground. Electric, water, sewer hookups, dump station, laundry, showers, fee area, 32 sites. Take CR 9 left.

DAVIS LAKE (milepost 243.1)

(877) 444-6777 (reservation service)   A US Forest Service-run campground.Electric, water, dump station, showers, fee area, 24 sites. 5 miles west of Parkway.

NATCHEZ TRACE RV PARK (milepost 251.6)

(662) 767-8609   Private campground. Electric, water, sewer hookups, dump station, laundry, pool, fee area. 22 sites, 13 pull-throughs, and 9 back-ins. Adjacent to Parkway on CR 506.

TRACE STATE PARK (milepost 259.7)

(662) 489-2958   Electric, water, dump station, showers, laundry, fee area, 52 sites, 3 pull-throughs and 49 back-ins. 7 miles from Parkway on MS 6, then 2 miles north.

TOMBIGBEE STATE PARK (milepost 263.6)

(662) 842-7669   Electric, water, dump station, sewer hookups, showers, fee area. 20 sites, back in only. US 78 East toward Tupelo, second exit, follow signs.

BARNES CROSSING (milepost 266.0)

(662) 844-6063   Private campground. Electric, water, sewer hookups, laundry, fee area. 50 sites,12 pull-throughs and 38 back-ins. One-half mile off Parkway on US 145 South.

WHIP-P.O.OR.-WILL (milepost 293.5)

(662) 728-2449   Electric, water, dump station, showers; fee area, 15 sites, 3 pull-throughs and 12 back-ins. 1 mile north to MS 4. Follow signs.

PINEY GROVE (milepost 293.5)

(662) 728-1134   An Army Corps of Engineers-owned camp-ground. Electric, water, dump station, showers, fee area. 141 sites, 13 pull-throughs and 128 back-ins. 1 mile north to MS 4, follow signs. Open mid-March–mid-November.

TISHOMINGO STATE PARK (milepost 303.9)

(662) 438-6914   Electric, water, dump station, showers, laundry, fee area. 62 sites, back-ins only. Adjacent to the Parkway.

DAVID CROCKETT STATE PARK (milepost 369.9)

(931) 762-9408   Electric, water, dump station, showers, pool, restaurant, fee area. 107 sites, back-ins only. 14 miles east on US 64.

MERIWETHER LEWIS (milepost 385.9)

No phone   A National Park Service-owned campground. No reservations, free of charge. Drinking water, hiking. 32 sites. On the Parkway.

FALL HOLLOW VILLAGE (milepost 391.9)

(931) 796-1480   Private campground. Electric, water, dump station, restaurant, store, bed-and-breakfast, fee area. West of the Parkway on US 412.

APPENDIX FOUR:
NATCHEZ TRACE PARKWAY SUB-DISTRICT OFFICES

Listed South to North

Note: With the exception of the Tupelo facility, these are not visitor contact stations, therefore there may not be a ranger on site at these locations. In an emergency call (800) 300-PARK (7275)

Natchez Sub-District (milepost 15.5)
Route 4, Box 250
Natchez, MS 39120
(601) 445-4211(all offices)

Port Gibson Sub-District (milepost 39.2)
1019 Highway 547
Port Gibson, MS 39150
(601) 437-5252

Ridgeland Sub-District (milepost 102.4)
100 East Jackson Street
Ridgeland, MS 39157
(601) 856-7321 (all offices)

Kosciusko Sub-District (milepost 159.7)
P.O. Box 416
Kosciusko, MS 39090
(601) 289-3671 (all offices)

Jeff Busby Site (milepost 193.1)
Route 3, Box 80-A
Ackerman, MS 39735
(601) 387-4365 (all offices)

Dancy Sub-District (milepost 214.5)
Route 1, Box 173
Mantee, MS 39751
(601) 263-5677

Tupelo Sub-District and Headquarters Area (milepost 266)
2680 Natchez Trace Parkway
Tupelo, MS 38804
(601) 680-4027

Cherokee Sub-District (milepost 320.3)
3204 Natchez Trace Parkway
Cherokee, AL 35616
(205) 359-6472 (maintenance)

Cherokee Sub-District (milepost 327.3)
3275 Natchez Trace Parkway
Cherokee, AL 35616
(205) 359-6372 (rangers)

Meriwether Lewis Sub-District (milepost 385.9)
191 Meriwether Lewis Park
Hohenwald, TN 38462
(931) 796-2675

Leipers Fork Sub-District (milepost 428.9)
5430 Pinewood Road
Franklin, TN 37064
(615) 790-9323

APPENDIX FIVE:

NON-VEHICULAR CAMPGROUNDS FOR BICYCLERS, HIKERS, AND SCOUT GROUPS

Kosciusko (milepost 159)
Enter the road marked District Ranger Office just south of the Kosciusko Information Center. On this road a tent symbol and arrow will direct you into the camping area on your right. Picnic tables, water, four tent pads, pit toilet, and fire grates are available.

Witch Dance (milepost 234)
Bicycle camping is permitted at the Witch Dance picnic area. Camping is to be done in the horse staging area to the west and south of the rest rooms. No camping is allowed in the picnic loop. Rest rooms, picnic tables fire grates, garbage cans, and water are available in the area.

Tupelo Visitor Center (milepost 266)
Bicycle camping is available at an outdoor classroom across the road from the Tupelo Visitor Center. Cross the Parkway at the south end of the Visitor Center parking lot, proceed through all four lanes of traffic, and continue on this road to the small parking area/ trailhead. Across the road from the parking area is a trail through the forest. Follow this trail to the camping area. Primitive cabins, fire grates, picnic tables, garbage cans, water, and pit toilets are available.

Colbert Ferry (milepost 327)
Enter the Colbert Ferry site, turn left, and follow the road to the left of the contact station, past the parking lot. Continue to the gated road marked with tent and bicycle symbols. Proceed through the gate and down the path to the right. Two tent sites, picnic tables, and fire grates are available. Water and rest rooms are located at the contact station.

Tennessee Highway 50 (milepost 408)
Follow the signs to the TN 50 trailhead of the Natchez Trace National Scenic Trail. This is a horse staging area. Water, picnic tables, fire grates, and garbage cans are available. Nearest rest rooms are at the Gordon House and Ferry Site just south of TN 50.

Index

. . . .

"Should we stop here?" To help you sort out your opt
into the following categories listed in ascending (sou